UNDERSTANDING
JOHN FOWLES

Understanding Contemporary British Literature
Matthew J. Bruccoli, General Editor

Understanding Graham Greene
by R. H. Miller

Understanding Doris Lessing
by Jean Pickering

Understanding Arnold Wesker
by Robert Wilcher

Understanding Kingsley Amis
by Merritt Moseley

Understanding Iris Murdoch
by Cheryl K. Bove

Understanding Paul West
by David W. Madden

Understanding John Fowles
by Thomas C. Foster

UNDERSTANDING

John
FOWLES

by THOMAS C. FOSTER

UNIVERSITY OF SOUTH CAROLINA PRESS

Published in Columbia, South Carolina, by the
University of South Carolina Press

Manufactured in the United States of America

Library of Congress Cataloging-in-Publication Data

Foster, Thomas C.
  Understanding John Fowles / by Thomas C. Foster
    p.   cm.—(Understanding contemporary British literature)
  Includes bibliographical references and index.
  Contents: Men, women, and novels—The collector, otherness,
obsession, and isolation—The magus and the existential dilemma—
The French lieutenant's woman, postmodern Victorian —The ebony
tower and mantissa, subjectivity and truth—Daniel Martin, the
mature Fowlesian novel—A maggot, narrative invention and
conventional storytelling—Conclusion.
  ISBN 1–57003–003–0
  1. Fowles, John, 1926– —Criticism and interpretation.
I. Title. II. Series.
PR6056.O85Z665 1994   94–3215
823'914–dc20

for Brenda

CONTENTS

Editor's Preface   ix

Chapter 1 Men, Women, and Novels   1

Chapter 2 *The Collector:* Otherness, Obsession, and Isolation   20

Chapter 3 *The Magus* and the Existential Dilemma   38

Chapter 4 *The French Lieutenant's Woman:* Postmodern Victorian   67

Chapter 5 *The Ebony Tower* and *Mantissa:* Subjectivity and Truth   91

Chapter 6 *Daniel Martin:* The Mature Fowlesian Novel   119

Chapter 7 *A Maggot:* Narrative Invention and Conventional Storytelling   140

Conclusion   168

Bibliography   171

Index   179

EDITOR'S PREFACE

The volumes of *Understanding Contemporary British Literature* have been planned as guides or companions for students as well as good nonacademic readers. The editor and publisher perceive a need for these volumes because much of the influential contemporary literature makes special demands. Uninitiated readers encounter difficulty in approaching works that depart from the traditional forms and techniques of prose and poetry. Literature relies on conventions, but the conventions keep evolving; new writers form their own conventions—which in time may become familiar. Put simply, *UCBL* provides instruction in how to read certain contemporary writers—identifying and explicating their material, themes, use of language, point of view, structures, symbolism, and responses to experience.

The word understanding in the titles was deliberately chosen. Many willing readers lack an adequate understanding of how contemporary literature works; that is, what the author is attempting to express and the means by which it is conveyed. Although the criticism and analysis in the series have been aimed at a level of general accessibility, these introductory volumes are meant to be applied in conjunction with the works they cover. They do not provide a substitute for the works and authors they introduce, but rather prepare the reader for more profitable literary experiences.

M. J. B.

UNDERSTANDING
JOHN FOWLES

CHAPTER ONE

Men, Women, and Novels

Career

John Fowles explores relationships: between men and women, between authors and characters, between writers and readers, between individual citizens and national character. In his life and his work he has insisted on individualism as the starting point for exploring those relationships. Not surprisingly, his characters have been solitaries and visionaries who operate outside the mainstream and who seek to make their own peace. He has written poetry, local history, philosophy, evocative nature and travel writing, literary reviews and appreciations, screenplays, and essays on travel, sport, war, and nature.

While his work has never been overtly autobiographical, his novels have drawn on personal experience for character details or initial situations. The Fowles family's wartime evacuation from Leigh-on-Sea, along the Thames, to rural Dorset, for instance, appears in the Dorset childhood in *Daniel Martin*

(1977). That novel also carries, through the title character's trade as screenwriter, traces of Fowles's unsatisfactory experiences with Hollywood in the adaptations of his first two novels. His early enthusiasm for butterfly collecting is shared by Ferdinand Clegg in *The Collector* (1963); after that novel, and in some measure as a result of it, Fowles gave up butterflies in favor of antique china and Victorian postcards.[1]

Born in 1926 in Leigh-on-Sea, Essex, he grew up in a comfortable suburban life, which, as an adult, he rejected for rural village life in Dorset. Like Fowles, several of his protagonists are products of public schools. Fowles attended Bedford School from 1939 to 1944, except for a term off following a nervous breakdown, and Oxford, after military service, during which he was stationed at Dartmoor in Devon, from 1945 to 1947. At Oxford (1947–1950) Fowles took a high second-class honors degree in French from New College, following which he lectured for a year at the University of Poitiers (1950–1951). He spent most of the next two years teaching on the Greek island of Spetsai, where he met his future wife, Elizabeth Whitton, whose marriage to a fellow master was faltering. His teaching experience at Anargyrios, a boys' school on Spetsai, is the base on which he builds the story of *The Magus* (1965), and his main character shares the author's dissatisfaction with the British style of education which the Greek school attempts to emulate.[2] After teaching on Spetsai, he returned to England, accepting for 1953–1954 a post at Ashridge Management College in Berkhamsted, Hertfordshire, where he taught adult education courses and became interested in the trade union and socialist positions held by a number of his students. He then taught at a private girls' school, St. Godric's College in Hampstead, London, until the success of *The Collector* in 1963 made it possible for him to give up teaching and write full-time.

His subsequent move to Lyme Regis, Dorset, provided material for *The French Lieutenant's Woman* (1969): his first home at Underhill Farm became "The Dairy" in the novel; the landscape and natural history feature prominently; and the celebrated vision of a Victorian woman's cloaked figure, the image that becomes Sarah Woodruff standing on the Cobb (the quay that snakes out into the sea), came to Fowles while he was living at Lyme. The move also fueled a career for him as a writer of local history. He has published several works about the Lyme area, most notably *A Short History of Lyme Regis* (1982) and the pamphlets *Lyme Regis: Three Town Walks* (1983), *Medieval Lyme Regis* (1984), and *A Brief History of Lyme* (1985). Fowles became a key member of the small community, including acting as curator of the Lyme Regis (Philpot) Museum from 1978 to 1988. His tenure as curator was ended by a mild stroke, which left him physically active but resulted in the end of his career as a novelist.[3] The landscapes and wild scenes of southwest England also figure prominently in *A Maggot* (1985).

Fowles has been a highly popular novelist since the beginning of his career. His first novel, *The Collector,* was published in 1963 by Jonathan Cape, the first publisher to whom he submitted it. The book's British sales were over 500,000 in the next two decades.[4] From that novel through *A Maggot,* Fowles has insisted on the radical autonomy of the individual, on the dangers of conformity, and on humanity's place in the natural world. His love of native English wildness shows up repeatedly in his fiction as well as in his efforts to preserve those remaining places of natural wild beauty, even to allowing his garden to revert to its own small wilderness.[5] He also seeks those wild places in individual human beings, those corners that have not been steamrolled into mindless conformity, and this wildness, too, he seeks to preserve in his fiction.

Overview

To a great extent John Fowles's novels form a single pattern of thought, concerned as they are with a cluster of formal, existential, intellectual, and emotional problems. The basic difficulty of relations between the sexes, issues of identity, the role of the artist in creating his work, freedom, morality, humanity's relation to nature—these themes and issues recur throughout his work. He says in his preface to the second edition of *The Aristos* (1970) that he had one chief concern in that work, "to preserve the freedom of the individual against all those pressures-to-conform that threaten our century" (7). The exploration of freedom remains central to his writing, from the horrors of captivity in *The Collector* to religious freethinking in *A Maggot*. In a sense this concern reflects Fowles's theological thinking, which may seem an odd strain of thought in a professed atheist.[6] But the problems of morality in a secular state are, for him, tied to problems of theology: if morality has, in the past, been based on God, then a new basis for morality must be located in a world without God, or a world in which God is so distant as to effectively not exist.

His humanism, then, grows out of a recognition that human beings are free to choose their course of action, that such freedom entails responsibilities, and that both freedom and responsibility must be explored and examined fully.

In *The Magus* Fowles creates a protagonist who is openly and very self-consciously existentialist, and he has said of *The French Lieutenant's Woman* that part of the attraction of the nineteenth century is that the Victorian age was highly existentialist, although it lacked the terminology to identify itself as such.[7] His male and female main characters in the novel are, as he asserts, existentialists before their time. In the rest of his fiction he has confronted the issues of existentialism time and again. In this strain of his thinking, particularly, Fowles shows himself to be in step with the major strain of European thought of his time, although here, as with everything he does, he develops a highly individual version. His sympathies are entirely with the atheistic existentialist school running from Friedrich Nietzsche through Martin Heidegger, Jean-Paul Sartre, and Albert Camus, rather than the religious strain of Søren Kierkegaard, Paul Tillich, and Martin Buber. Several major elements of European existentialism appear in Fowles's work: alienation, absurdity, freedom.

Foremost among them is alienation. Social and economic factors since the beginning of the Industrial Revolution have acted to drive human beings away from one another, from God, from nature, and ultimately from their own true selves.[8] At the same time, overwhelming force has been brought to bear by governments against the autonomy of the Self in an effort to minimize individuality and create conformity. This is what Fowles means in *The Aristos* when he says that "all states and societies are incipiently fascist" (121); in other words, the goals of the state and the individual are antithetical, and the state seeks to crush the individual. Eventually, one is alienated from the whole of that society and even from oneself. He concludes that the proper corrective to fascism is not socialism (although he has sympathies with its social goals) but, rather, existentialism, by which he means a radical assertion of the Self. Alienation is the standard starting point of a Fowlesian novel or story: the hero, who is male, is cut off from his fellow human beings, out of step with his society, and at odds with his own true Self. He finds no refuge, no place of solace, no source of easy answers in his world. Often he meets a woman who shares or mirrors his difficulties, but with the added difficulty that she lives in a society that values her individuality even less because of gender. His protagonists are cut off by virtue of class (Charles Smithson as part of the dying aristocracy in an increasingly middle-class Victorian England in *The French Lieutenant's Woman),* education (the critic in "Poor Koko" who cannot relate to his working-class captor), occupation (Mike Jennings is a police detective—a person who provokes suspicion or resentment in others—in "The Enigma"), or sensibility (Nicholas Urfe's pose as sensitive and alienated poet in *The Magus).* His most spectacular instance of alienation, though, contains all these elements, plus the distancing factor of gender: Sarah Woodruff in *The French Lieutenant's Woman.* Not only is she totally alienated from society, God, and self, but she realizes, unlike Charles Smithson, the absurdity of her situation.

Absurdity is the second of the major components of existentialism which appear in Fowles. By absurdity, what he calls "the nemo," he means the recognition of the inconsequence of one's existence, which is at odds with one's aspirations. At its

MEN, WOMEN, AND NOVELS

most basic, the absurdist moment occurs when one's desire to live forever clashes with one's recognition that one will die and that one is helpless to change that outcome. "The nemo," he says, "is man's sense of his own futility and ephemerality; of his relativity, his comparativeness, of his virtual nothingness" (*Aristos,* 49). Fowles identifies the nemo as the fourth part of the psyche, in addition to the ego, id, and superego; it is the state of negation, the condition of being aware of being nobody. At the same time, the individual is filled with angst, or anxiety, because of a sudden awareness of freedom. Finding himself cut off from the many, from the world of "They," he becomes an "I" who cannot rely on received information or rules—what is known as living in "bad faith"—and who must therefore make all decisions for himself, with no guidance from without. The individual will experience unspecified, nameless fear, the "fear and trembling" that existentialists speak of as angst.[9] This condition of being nobody and at the same time isolated from the herd is itself an absurd situation. Deeply enough felt, absurdity leads to an awareness of, even a desire for, nonbeing.

Indeed, this existential misery appears in Fowles's fiction chiefly as an impulse toward suicide. Character after character confronts the suicidal moment, filled with anxiety and awareness of absurdity, only to pull back at the last moment. Nicholas Urfe, for instance, goes off into the woods to shoot himself, but does not. Sarah Woodruff stands at her window, in the literal dark night of her soul, preparing to jump, but she does not. Charles Smithson, too, has a moment in which he is tempted by suicide. The central disappearances in "The Enigma" and *A Maggot* may have been suicides and are at least briefly considered as such. Of the major characters only Catherine in "The Cloud" clearly yields to suicidal despair. Like Sarah, her alienation and sense of absurdity have manifold sources: grief at the death of her husband, dissatisfactions with male domination (including sexual exploitation), unresolvable differences of sensibility from her surrounding society, anxiety resulting from being cut off from the mass of They through her loss. She has, in other words, a full slate of reasons for being alienated and anxious, and for finding her life and situation absurd. Whether her suicide is an assertion of freedom or a yielding to despair remains an open question. Certainly, the existentialism of Albert Camus, for instance, would argue that suicide seizes not real freedom but merely the illusion of freedom, which the victim mistakes in her anxious state.[10] Yet Fowles is not a philosopher but a novelist. His handling of Catherine's removal from the story explores the full range of dramatic as well as philosophical possibilities. Her suicide may or may not have to do with an assertion of freedom. It may form a "text" of its own, a message back to those living, or it may bring the text of her story to closure; she has already told a story to her niece which sheds light on her situation, and this may be the only possible remaining step for her. The source of the act may be defiance, despair, grief, or love. Fowles's novelistic instincts, here as elsewhere, are stronger than any programmatic loyalty to existentialism, and the resulting ambiguity of Catherine's ending is truer to the story than to a philosophical movement.

Perhaps the greatest source of anxiety and misery in existentialism is freedom. The term *freedom* causes a great deal of confusion for Americans, in particular, because of the emphasis in the Anglo-American tradition on freedom. Yet the agrarian independence of Jeffersonian democracy, with its stress on individual liberties and the absence of interference from the state, has little to do with the existentialists' notion of freedom. Among these philosophers freedom is itself a cause of anxiety, since freedom is constituted by absence: of divine control, of operative societal norms, of received morality. The individual, having broken loose from the herd, is free to the extent that no one is watching his actions or that no one cares. Fowles writes in *The Aristos,* and elsewhere, of the sign of God being His absence, that the truly omnipotent creator would not meddle in day-to-day issues of existence, that any creator's second act would be to abscond (19, 22–28). Miranda realizes during her captivity in *The Collector* that, even if God exists, his effect on her is so nonexistent that she is effectively alone. Fowles expresses the situation most clearly in *The French Lieutenant's Woman,* in connection with Charles's having to choose the right course of action for himself: "He had not the benefit of existentialist terminology; but what he felt was really a very clear case of the anxiety of freedom—that is, the realization that one *is* free and the realization that being free is a situation of terror."[11] Charles is simultaneously excited and appalled at being forced to exercise moral choice, and he is unsettled by the lack of received information, or of the utility of that information. Ultimately, only he can choose whether to go to Sarah, thereby flying in the face of convention and propriety, or to return to Ernestina. Fowlesian protagonists must each meet their moment of choice alone, both morally and dramatically, for the novelist typically depopulates his stage during moments of great personal crisis. Daniel Martin, for instance, must choose between Jane and Jenny when neither is present. Similarly, Nicholas Urfe reaches his important decisions while alone, and indeed one of the functions of Conchis's externalized drama is to isolate Nicholas so he can decide. Freedom is intimately tied to separation from the mass of They, since humans can only be free, and aware of their freedom, singly.

One is never tempted with Fowles, however, as one may be with Camus or Sartre, to see the fiction as a mere working out of the philosophy, as a didactic exercise, because his existentialist leanings form only one part of his fictional enterprise. An equally important base is his interest in romance. Like the medieval romance, the quest plays a large role in his fiction. His two best-known heroes, Nicholas Urfe and Charles Smithson, are Fowlesian knights-errant, questers after something only vaguely defined and not always clear to the heroes. Their errands are rarely so well defined as those of Marie de France or the Arthurian legends, although the result is familiar. It can be argued that the ultimate goal of all quest literature, from the Grail stories through the movie *Star Wars,* is self-knowledge. The quester is stripped of his social support system and forced to rely on his own wits, his own resourcefulness, his own moral vision. In the process of fighting his way through alien and hostile terrain, he must come to grips with his own identity and his own limitations, completing the maturing process. The quester has traditionally been a young man, not yet married or settled in society, often newly knighted. So too with Fowles, whose protagonists are generally in early adulthood, still on the threshold of, and not yet reconciled to, adult responsibilities.

The paths of these quests lead through wildernesses of romantic entanglement and narcissistic excess. Sexual relations range from the decidedly strained (*The French Lieutenant's*

Woman) to the violent *(The Collector),* from the coy *(The Ebony Tower* [1974]) to the bizarre *(A Maggot).* Somewhere behind all these struggles lies the warfare of a male novelist with his muse, a cockeyed version of which makes up the substance of *Mantissa.* His men often find (or fail to find) their way through the contrast between a "realistic" woman and a mysterious muse-enchant-ress: Ernestina-Sarah for Charles Smithson, Alison-Julie for Nicholas Urfe. Fowles places great emphasis on "Otherness" and on the difficulty, even the impossibility, of knowing the "Other"— a person outside the Self whose presence helps to define the Self and its limits. At the same time, that fascination with Otherness, with the dichotomies and dilemmas of the opposite sex, often only demonstrates, as in *Daniel Martin,* the oppositions within individual identity.

The source of the Other for Fowles, ultimately, is Jungian psychology. The concept of the Other shows up in existentialism as well, as any manifestation of the "not-I" and chiefly as a source of peril for the Self if it interprets itself through the eyes of the Other.[12] Still, the greatest affinity is with Jung, whose thought shows up in a host of ways in Fowles's fiction, particularly in the use of archetypal characters and situations and in the anima-animus dichotomy—the opposed pairing of purely female and purely male attributes. The sources of Otherness are not simply psychological, relying as they do also on class, educational, and generational differences. Yet the main division between Self and Other, at least as Fowles employs them, rests on gender distinc-tion, between the questing male protagonist and the mysterious (to him, at least) female, whose silence and incomprehensibility spurs him to action. In Jung among the host of dualities—light/ dark, positive/negative, day/night, conscious/unconscious—

which inform existence, the male/female is perhaps decisive. As Edward Whitmont explains, this duality goes right to the center of being:

> Anima and animus are the archetypes of what for either sex is the *totally* other. Each represents a world that is at first quite incomprehensible to its opposite, a world that can never be directly known. Even though we carry within us elements of the opposite sex, their field of expression is precisely that area which is most obscure, strange, irrational, and fear-inspiring to us; it can be intuited and "felt out" but never completely understood. . . . [T]here is nothing so totally "other" as the opposite sex.[13]

That is to say, because the differences between men and women are so thoroughgoing, they can never really understand each other fully. Therefore, the most alien person one human being can experience is a member of the opposite sex. Since the protagonists and even the narrative voices in his novels are overwhelmingly male, Fowles focuses on the anima (the female archetype) as the chief Other. His heroes, in the midst of strongly male quests, must try to come to terms with what is essentially unknowable, and this paradoxical situation brings them up short. In their baffling confrontations with representatives of nearly pure anima (that is, strongly female characters), they must also confront issues of their own identity and behavior. Such encounters carry with them both an element of terror and the possibility of creative inspiration.

The protagonists are not uniformly successful in meeting and understanding the Other. In *The Collector* Frederick Clegg never comprehends Miranda because he never meets her; his fantasy image of her is so strong that her reality cannot break through. Not surprisingly, Clegg's fantasy proves disastrous for Miranda while providing no self-illumination for him. Other protagonists from Nicholas Urfe of *The Magus* to Henry Ayscough of *A Maggot* find their encounters with the Other unsettling, mystifying, and provocative both sexually and creatively. Driven initially by sexual desire in these encounters, the men are goaded to changes in their lives, their work, their understanding of themselves. Such changes may not be pleasant, as when David Williams of "The Ebony Tower" fails to rescue Diana or to undergo personal growth, yet even here the possibility has existed and come his way through his meeting with Diana as archetypal female. The notion of Otherness features in Fowles's fiction also in the class and generational warfare of "Poor Koko" and even in the tensions between Nicholas Urfe and Maurice Conchis in *The Magus*. Still, it is in the wilderness of gender and sexuality that the concept really flourishes.

Fowles has sometimes been criticized for his treatment of women in his novels. Pamela Cooper, for instance, sees Fowles, even in *A Maggot,* "still portraying women not so much as individuals but as fantasies, the incarnations of a timeless femininity."[14] To be sure, his interest in the romance, his exploration of woman as the Other, his deployment of Jungian thinking generally (with its stress on archetypes), and his detailed exploration of male consciousness all lead him to depict his female characters as less than, or perhaps more than, realistic. He says as much in discussing *The French Lieutenant's Woman:* "My female characters tend to dominate the male. I see man as a kind of artifice, and woman as a kind of reality. the one is cold idea, the other is warm fact. Daedalus faces Venus, and Venus must win."[15] He goes on to say that, had he been able to overcome the technical difficulties, he would have liked to make Maurice Conchis in *The Magus* a woman. As it is, he projects much of Conchis's gamesmanship and power onto Julie and, later, onto her mother, Mme de Seitas. What he reveals here is that his view of women is highly traditional and not especially in step with contemporary feminism. Cooper is correct in her assertions that his women wind up in secondary roles, not as the artist or master but, instead, as his model or helper. Yet that may reflect historical accuracy on his part rather than nefarious male power games. The options available to Sarah in the middle of the nineteenth century or to Rebecca in the middle of the previous century in *A Maggot* would be extremely limited; indeed, those limitations go far in explaining how the two come to be in their initial predicaments. Even in *Daniel Martin* Fowles is dealing with a generation brought up to believe that women were destined for home and family, for supporting roles. His efforts have generally been directed at changing male attitudes toward women from selfish and criminal objectification in *The Collector* and *The Magus* to a fuller understanding and appreciation in *Daniel Martin* or *A Maggot*. And the women he presents, while secondary characters for the most part, have ranged from the subservient Diana in "The Ebony Tower" to the highly outspoken Rebecca Hocknell and the strong-willed Sarah Woodruff.

While issues of character and philosophy form a locus of concern in the fiction, there is also an interest in the role of art and the artist. Fowles is simultaneously a postmodernist *and* a traditionalist, presenting experimentation with a human face. His influences range from medieval romances of Marie de France

MEN, WOMEN, AND NOVELS

and Chrétien de Troyes to the great Victorian novelists, Thomas Hardy in particular, to the narrative theories of Roland Barthes and Alain Robbe-Grillet, to identify only a few. Certainly, Henri Alain-Fournier's *Le Grand Meaulnes* has a major impact on his fiction, especially the stories in *The Ebony Tower,* while the profligate inventiveness of Flann O'Brien's work, which often calls attention to the fictionality of the enterprise, can be seen in *Mantissa.* Still, for all the talk of influences, there is never a sense in Fowles that the influences are the work. Rather, he imports, distorts, and exploits, using his sources for his own ends. One may say, for instance, that Marie de France's *Eliduc* informs his novella "The Ebony Tower," yet his reworking is ironic, showing how far modern love has fallen from the courtly. Marie would scarcely recognize her story in his. The ironic inversion is such that Fowles includes a translation of *Eliduc* immediately after his novella, inviting readers to compare the two. This reworking of earlier materials is typical of his work. In *The French Lieutenant's Woman* he reworks the materials of the Victorian novel, yet the result is neither a true Victorian novel nor a parody of one. He has produced, instead, a contemporary work that uses the form of the Victorian novel ironically to achieve its ends. It calls attention to the ways in which it could not be by Hardy or George Eliot, and the act of calling attention to itself announces that it is not a Victorian novel.

Strategies of this sort go by various names among critics and writers: self-referentiality, reflexivity, and metafiction, often used interchangeably, for metafictional works are highly self-referential, or self-reflexive, turning back on themselves to examine their own processes of creation. The term *metafiction* seems to have been coined by novelist and theorist William Gass in 1970 in his *Fiction and the Figures of Life*. At that time the term was being applied to writers of the avant-garde: Jorge Luis Borges, Flann O'Brien, Vladimir Nabokov, John Barth, Italo Calvino, Robert Coover, and John Hawkes as well as Gass and Fowles. Since then it has come to be seen by some critics as a tendency that lies within all fiction. *Metafiction,* according to Patricia Waugh, "is a term given to fictional writing which self-consciously and syntactically draws attention to its status as artefact in order to pose questions about the relationship between fiction and reality."[16] Using the theories of Mikhail Bakhtin, Waugh explores the notion that all fiction has a "dialogic potential," a conflict between the fictional work's effort at representation and the impulse to examine that effort. Realism is distinguished by its suppression of this dialogue, by its thoroughgoing insistence on representation and resistance to examining or undermining the illusion of mimesis. Works one would call metafictional, on the other hand, simultaneously create the fictional illusion and lay it bare, calling attention to its illusory quality.[17] Jerome Klinkowitz offers a useful distinction in his terms *transparent* and *opaque.* For him works of realism or naturalism strive for transparency, that is, for the status of invisible conveyors of the story. Readers look directly through the package to its contents. The metafictional, or postmodern, novel, on the contrary, is opaque in the sense that its presence cannot be ignored or looked through; it calls attention to itself.

Whichever term is employed, this self-conscious fiction reveals its own artifice and, by so doing, reveals also the artifice that realism seeks to hide from readers. Waugh notes that realism often supplies the background "against which experimental strategies can foreground themselves."[18] Those strategies may

MEN, WOMEN, AND NOVELS

include what Bakhtin refers to as parody, the conscious use and undermining of previous literary forms, most clearly evident in *The French Lieutenant's Woman* and *A Maggot,* as well as the self-begetting novel, such as *Daniel Martin,* in which the progress of the narrative is toward the moment at which the novel we are reading can be written. Fowles frequently points out that he is engaged in creating a literary artifact as well as in giving narrative duties to his characters, who use their own stories to teach or convert other characters. The magical abilities of his Magus are largely narrative. The net result of these strategies is to remind readers of the uses to which narrative can be put and the fictiveness of his whole enterprise.

What sets Fowles apart from many metafictionists is his love of storytelling. While he does place the conflict between creating the illusion and laying it bare in the foreground, he takes great care to create a masterful illusion. He shares with his Victorian forebears a belief in the power of story to engage readers. Rarely, then, does his fiction simply devolve into a cold exercise in experimentalism, as it does with many postmodernists. Perhaps only *Mantissa* contains this failing and then largely in the service of comedy. In his other work he offers stories and characters that readers find deeply engaging, while at the same time he explores the limitations of conventional storytelling. Like Borges or Nabokov, he demonstrates a belief that any story contains all possible stories, the labyrinthine "garden of forking paths" which Borges writes about. His fiction, then, often ends indeterminately or ambiguously, inviting the reader to become involved in the resolution. Which ending of *The French Lieutenant's Woman* does the reader choose? What happens after the frozen moment at the end of *The Magus?* In order for readers to enter into these resolutions they must care deeply about the foregoing stories, enough that they want to finish the novels according to their own lights. This belief that fiction should engage readers dramatically and morally even in the midst of experimentation has made Fowles into that rarity, the critically successful serious novelist who also enjoys wide general readership.

John Fowles bridges the void between traditional narrative and postmodern experiment, between philosophical meditation and fictional extravaganza, between realism and fantasy, between personal freedom and social responsibility. His continuing popularity attests to the success of his enterprise. More important, his work remains vital, capable of surprising us in its variety and inventiveness, while impressing us with its continuing intellectual and moral seriousness. An expansive talent, he writes novels readers can lose themselves in—and, perhaps, thereby find themselves as well.

Notes

1. Carol M. Barnum, "John Fowles," in *Critical Survey of Long Fiction,* English language edition, ed. Frank N. Magill (Englewood Cliffs, N.J.: Salem, 1983) 1010.

2. James R. Aubrey, *John Fowles: A Reference Companion* (New York: Greenwood, 1991) 18.

3. Aubrey 30.

4. Simon Loveday, *The Romances of John Fowles* (New York: St. Martin's, 1985) xii.

5. Aubrey 26, 32–34.

6. In *The Aristos* he says he is not an atheist but must act in all outward ways as if he is (26). By the time he writes *A Maggot* (Boston: Little, Brown, 1985), he refers to himself as "a convinced atheist" (462). I think it reasonable to conclude, given the context—an epilogue that steps outside the narrative frame of the novel—that in the latter case he is speaking in his own voice rather than as a narrative character.

7. Fowles, "Notes on an Unfinished Novel," in *Afterwords: Novelists on Their Novels,* ed. Thomas McCormack (New York: Harper, 1969) 165–66.

8. Gordon Bigelow, "A Primer of Existentialism," *College English* Dec. 1961, 171–78.

9. David E. Cooper, *Existentialism: A Reconstruction* (Cambridge, Mass.: Basil Blackwell, 1990) 127–33.

10. Albert Camus, *The Myth of Sisyphus,* trans. Justin O'Brien (New York: Penguin, 1986) 54–58.

11. Fowles, *The French Lieutenant's Woman* (Boston: Little, Brown, 1969) 267. Subsequent references will be noted parenthetically.

12. Ernst Breisach, *Introduction to Modern Existentialism* (New York: Grove, 1962) 224–29. See also Cooper 117–24.

13. Edward C. Whitmont, *The Symbolic Quest: Basic Concepts in Analytic Psychology* (New York: Harper, 1969) 185.

14. Pamela Cooper, *The Fictions of John Fowles: Power, Creativity, Femininity* (Ottawa: U of Ottawa P, 1991) 218.

15. "Notes on an Unfinished Novel," 172.

16. Patricia Waugh, *Metafiction: The Theory and Practice of Self-Conscious Fiction* (London: Routledge, 1984) 2.

17. Waugh 5–6.

18. Waugh 18.

CHAPTER TWO

The Collector: **Otherness, Obsession, and Isolation**

John Fowles burst onto the literary scene with his first published novel, *The Collector,* in 1963. While it shares concerns and themes with his later novels, in many ways the book is an anomaly in his oeuvre. Whereas *The French Lieutenant's Woman* exploits the form of the Victorian novel and *The Magus* exploits the form of the thriller, *The Collector* is a thriller. To be sure, it pushes the boundaries of the genre, and is a highly literary instance, but its intent is to be a thriller. The genre-fiction element sets the book apart, as does the odious nature of the male protagonist. Other Fowlesian men, particularly Nicholas Urfe in *The Magus* and David Williams in "The Ebony Tower," will be considerably less than heroic, but Ferdinand Clegg stands alone as an out-and-out madman and villain.

In part these unusual qualities in the novel can be attributed to its period of composition. The late 1950s and early 1960s saw a considerable number of sociopathic protagonists and antiheroes in fiction and drama, from the small-time hustlers and petty criminals of the American Beat writers through the "angry young men" of British novels and plays. Fowles even refers to one of the principal "angry" writers, Alan Sillitoe, when Miranda Grey reads, disapprovingly, *Saturday Night and Sunday Morning*—although, in terms of its themes of isolation and captivity, *The Loneliness of the Long-Distance Runner* would be a more exact comparison. Miranda dislikes Sillitoe's novel chiefly because of its hero's antipathy to societal norms and, especially, to art and culture.

The Collector, like Anthony Burgess's *Clockwork Orange* or Vladimir Nabokov's *Lolita,* is an exercise in point of view, an attempt to make heinous crimes and moral monsters sufficiently palatable that readers can finish reading the novels that detail them. All three novels revolve around protagonists with seriously distorted views of right and wrong, and in a sense all of them use those protagonists to indict the society that contains them, since they are more representative figures than readers might care to believe. What all of these novels point to is a breakdown of the ethical, spiritual, and cultural systems in the society they portray. Fowles makes this point specifically when he has Miranda, writing in her journal, deride the "New People"—the materialistic, upwardly mobile members of the working and lower classes who are destroying the culture and the landscape, who are happy with their cars and their televisions, and who are taking over from the formerly stable privileged classes. Social upheaval, then, lies to a large degree behind the creation of these unsavory main characters.

Clegg, however, differs from these other characters in one important respect: he is utterly lacking in charm. Burgess and Nabokov, especially, try to win readers over with their protagonists' personal style and linguistic elegance. Clegg possesses no such linguistic or personal charm. Indeed, he is inhibited, passive, denying, utterly lacking in self-awareness, and nearly inarticulate. He cannot mention sex, for instance, except as "the other thing," although there are many other things in his narrative which he refers to as "the other thing" as well. Whereas Alex or Humbert choose their analogies and descriptions with care, putting the best face on their crimes, Clegg is woefully inept. He does not understand that comparing his capture of Miranda to collecting a rare butterfly, as he does—the "Queen of Spain Fritillary"—far from excusing the act, underscores the inhuman view he has of her and the deadly nature of the kidnapping, since butterflies must be killed to be collected. Nor does he realize what he is revealing when he says he has been learning techniques from reading *Secrets of the Gestapo*. Readers may view him with a certain fascination, but they are in no danger of being won over to his point of view.

Ferdinand (real name, Frederick) Clegg may be the most bizarrely passive kidnapper in literature. He sees himself as a victim, the world as the aggressor. Much in his past supports his view: his father died while driving drunk when young Fred was two, and shortly after that his mother ran off, leaving him with his Aunt Annie and her wheelchair-bound daughter, Mabel, both of whom are inhibited, judgmental, and bitter. Working as a very minor functionary in a government office, he finds his life suddenly changed when he wins the football pools for over seventy-three thousand pounds. When he gives five hundred pounds to his former coworkers, he says of their thank-you notes, "You could see they thought I was mean."[1] This observation is typical of him: he professes to be satisfied with himself but projects his insecurities and neuroses onto others' views of him. He never claims to be worried that he may be mad, suggesting, instead, that it is others who treat him like a madman. At some very deep, repressed level Clegg knows something is terribly wrong with him, yet he can never admit it. Rather, he permits himself to see the world as the source of his trouble, his own self-disgust mirrored (and thereby disguised) in another's eyes. Even with his major act, the kidnapping, he takes a passive view of his role. The whole time he is buying and outfitting his isolated cottage for the kidnapping, he denies that he is serious about his plans. And he attempts to deny that his obsession is unusual, arguing that many people would do what he did if they had the money and time, that only poverty keeps them in line. Waiting for her, he says he may have wanted to let fate stop him, that he felt as if he were being swept along by a current he could not control. He completely overlooks the fact that he, and no one else, created that current.

His passivity extends into the sexual arena as well. Early on he says he has never had what girls look for and cannot understand why his coarse, aggressive coworker, Crutchley, is sexually successful. Yet any manifestation of female sexuality disgusts Clegg. His one sexual experience, an assignation with a prostitute, proved unsuccessful; typically, he chalks his impotence up to her being "horrible." Miranda's use of obscenity appalls him, and any display of sexuality puts him off. When in a final desperate act she strips and attempts to seduce him, he loses all respect for her. He says he could get "that," meaning sex, by going to a prostitute. Even his fantasies of marriage to her are completely free of sex: they are partners in life, in butterfly collecting, in art, but not in bed. Of course, his sexual difficulties are largely a result of his hatred of women. He deeply resents his absconding mother, saying that, even if she is alive, he does not want to meet her. He dislikes his Aunt Annie and Mabel and resents being stuck with them. At the first opportunity he ships them off to Australia (and out of his story) to visit relatives. Of Miranda he says at one point that her behavior, switching moods from gaiety to spite in a moment, "is just like a woman." He neglects the fact that her mood swings might have something to do with being held against her will. He never really understands Miranda as a human being in her own right; if he did, of course, he could not cage her as he does. Instead, he sees her as representative of womankind—young student, nun, whore, harpy, or princess, by turns. Yet none of the versions is a complete person, and none of them includes a healthy sexual identity.

Of those views the dominant one, or at any rate the one Clegg wishes to be dominant, is of the captive princess. Miranda has the disconcerting habit of not cooperating, that is, not playing the role. The story he imagines for himself and his conquest is one Fowles returns to time and again, *la princesse lointaine,* the beautiful captive in the tower. In the present case, however, Clegg has unwittingly inverted the myth from the outset by locking her not in a tower but, instead, in a cave. His attempts, moreover, to play the gallant prince are upended by his also having to be the jailing ogre. Despite his fondest wishes, fairy tales are not organized for individuals to play multiple parts, as he must from the start. Before he captures her he dreams first of rescuing her from an attacker then finds his dream changed so that he is the attacker. One moment Ferdinand delights in buying nice things that Miranda has requested, the next he is thwarting another escape attempt. In one way or another virtually all of Fowles's later heroes are questing knights, seeking to save damsels in distress and gaining (often inadvertently) self-knowledge. Clegg fails to see that one cannot be the agent of salvation as well as the agent of distress.

In part this visionary failure is due to a more basic oversight having to do with the nature of the fairy tale itself: the captured princess, in every story, seeks constantly, and solely, for escape. He has assumed that the captive is more or less satisfied with or resigned to her state, that she suffers captivity passively until a rescuer boldly enters the tower and carts her off, itself a sort of kidnapping. He is therefore surprised at Miranda's ceaseless attempts at escape and at the energy and sometimes the violence of her efforts. If she attempts to win him over with kindness, or soften him up with sex, she also strikes him with a hatchet and tries to dig out with a nail. His fairy tale can never come true, chiefly because the facts do not fit the fancy, because the real story misses the myth by a considerable difference.

It also fails, chillingly, because Clegg is incapable of self-knowledge, which is the ultimate result, if not the stated goal, of every successful quest. The knight-errant may or may not return with his Grail, but he returns more mature, more knowledgeable, and more self-aware. He has encountered sin, doubt, fear, and temptation, and he has come through. Clegg encounters them and is unmoved. Carol Barnum sees *The Collector* as the reversal of quest myths operative in Fowles's other works and Clegg as the dark mirror image of Nicholas Urfe.[2] Whereas the quester assumes adult responsibility, Clegg is stuck in the juvenile pattern of blaming others. When he arrives at the end of the novel, considering (and denying that he is considering) another victim, the readers' horror is not one of shocked surprise but, rather, of familiarity: of course he will do it again. He has learned nothing from his first escapade.

Miranda Grey represents everything that Clegg lacks. She is beautiful, talented, well-off financially, popular, confident. Indeed, it is the collection of these traits which makes her initially attractive to him, because she is such a rarity in his world. She is dedicated to nonviolence and is appalled at his butterfly collecting. Her very definite views on art and taste lead her to despise everything Clegg attempts in the way of clothing and decor, even to the point of rejecting his interest in photography as freezing, or "killing," its subject. Perhaps the biggest difference between them, aside from gender, is the class distinction. Miranda is the daughter of a doctor; many of her traits have to do with her upper-middle-class background, and she takes her privilege largely for granted. When Clegg criticizes Piers as a "loud noisy public-school type with a sports car," his complaint is dripping with the envy of one who has been closed out of that world. When Miranda refers to him as being a stupid public school boy, she makes her judgment from a base of personal experience, having known other boys from Stowe (Piers's school) and from other public schools.

Just as Clegg fails to recognize his bitterness, resentment, and suspicion as functions of his class situation, so Miranda fails to see her own views and limitations as class based. Less than two weeks after her kidnapping they have an argument about the hydrogen bomb. Through the entire conversation she acts smugly superior, asserting that her views are the only views and that, if good and "decent" people object to the Bomb, the government will have to do something about it. She belittles Clegg's view that his feelings on the subject make no difference, largely because she is from a class that believes it can make a difference, from which government leaders come and to which they must therefore listen. She has no patience with his lower-class sense of futility or with his objections to pacifism, since she assumes that all good people are, like her, pacifists.

Her literary comparisons are by-products of her background. A lower-class woman reading Jane Austen is not likely to say, as Miranda does, "I am Emma Woodhouse" (146). She compares herself, too, to George Bernard Shaw's Major Barbara, who, like Miranda, can indulge her social improvement interests because she comes from a wealthy, safe background (although Miranda fails to see this part of the comparison). Her lack of sympathy for Sillitoe's Arthur Seaton is largely class based as well, since she cannot imagine her way into Arthur's world. Even her nickname for Clegg, Caliban, demonstrates her educational privilege. Clegg has no sense that, in changing his own name and then kidnapping her, he has brought together the names of the young lovers in *The Tempest*. Miranda, on the other hand, has read her Shakespeare, and turns Ferdinand, the lover, into Caliban, the savage, the monster, the would-be rapist. Her literary and artistic leanings have to do more with being born into the "right" class than with any overwhelming talent or fire of inspiration burning inside her. At one point she writes in her journal that she is one of the artistic few, but then in her next entry she says she merely wishes to be one of them, a wish she has always, until her kidnapping, been able to indulge.

The class war between the two leads to a consideration in the novel regarding the question of England, a concern that will run through Fowles's subsequent fiction. The question is not, as in E. M. Forster's *Howards End,* who shall inherit England—that was a question for an earlier generation. Instead, it is very much a postcolonial, postwar, late industrial age question: What is England that anyone would want to inherit it or to live there? He will return to this issue in *Daniel Martin.* Miranda comes very close to speaking for her creator when she decries the genteel world of her parents as conformist, comfortable, philistine, and smug. Yet she hates even more Clegg's England, which she sees as a "miserable Nonconformist suburban" world filled with "blindness, deadness, out-of-dateness, stodginess and, yes, sheer jealous malice" (151)—what she calls England's Calibanity.

This assessment, though, proves to be a sticking point in the novel, for, while Fowles shows what he dislikes about England, he does not show the England he does admire. In part this has to do with the subject matter: the story closes out positive possibilities, wholesome alternatives. In general, the author is not terribly enthusiastic about social England in any class, although he believes in the possibility of individual redemption. Rather, he leans toward mythic England, "the old green England" of Robin Hood legends and Thomas Hardy's novels. His boyhood move to Dorset during wartime and his adult years in Lyme Regis show up in his novels, in which contact with nature becomes a kind of golden moment irreproducible in a social setting. Of course, a novel set principally in a dungeon cannot achieve such golden moments of communing with the greenwood. *The Collector,* then, sets up an issue whose resolution must be delayed for later consideration.

In describing her battles with Clegg and thinking over her own situation, Miranda swings between moods of optimism and despair, plotting and resignation, as she tells her side of the tale. Her narrative, in the form of personal journal entries running from 14 October to 7 December, is highly reactive in nature, as indeed journals tend to be. Her entries are typically written at the end of an episode, so that she is telling of what has happened, often in its immediate aftermath, when her emotions are still seething. As 14 November, the promised release date, approaches, she allows herself to feel hope then goes on a hunger strike for five days when he reneges on his promise. Knowing that he can never let her go because his crime would be found out, she nevertheless devises schemes by which he will set her free, only to have her hopes dashed time after time. Miranda's narrative lacks clear overall structure because it is day-to-day in nature; that is to say, she has no large-scale plan, no organizational design larger than the day's telling. This lack of structure is common to the journal and epistolary narrative, of course, and from the eighteenth century such novels have required readers to assemble the entries and see the design that eludes the character-narrators. Such a narrative strategy fits Miranda's situation, since a captive cannot see the larger design, cannot grasp the whole working of the story, shut away as she is in her tiny space. Miranda's most famous predecessor, Samuel Richardson's Clarissa Harlow, has her story told in letter form as well.

The choice of narrative approach for Miranda and Ferdinand points to Fowles's already established concern with the shape of storytelling. As in his later novels, the technical aspects of form grow out of (or dictate, since causality is difficult to determine exactly) the demands of subject and theme. His approach in *The*

UNDERSTANDING JOHN FOWLES

Collector is to tell the same story from two different viewpoints, that of the kidnapper and that of his victim. Clegg's telling incorporates more information, fuller understanding of the background and events, and explanation of motives (insofar as he can understand them himself) of the perpetrator. What he lacks is any comprehension of Miranda. Miranda, for her part, can supply what he lacks about her as well as offer a differing perspective on him. Indeed, because Clegg is so lacking in self-awareness, he proves to be a very poor observer of himself. The best he can do, often, is to describe the disgust he thinks he perceives in others. Miranda can describe his movements, his gestures, his tone of voice, and his conversational gambits better than he can. At the same time, of necessity she cannot tell everything. She can only describe her dying up to the point at which she is too weak to continue writing, so from there on Clegg must take over again. Moreover, the shapelessness of her narrative, required in the interest of verisimilitude, makes the journals a poor choice of device with which to begin the novel.

Fowles is obliged to follow the logic of the action and of its narrative devices in structuring his novel, beginning with Clegg's overarching version then switching to the more impressionistic and fragmentary style of Miranda's journals and then back to his wheedling and self-justification after she dies. This strategy affords him the chance to cover the same territory twice, from two radically different viewpoints. Already knowing the outcomes from Clegg's earlier narrative, readers watch her stratagems for escape as, one by one, they are built and then destroyed. In the third part Clegg covers information first brought up in the journals, and, indeed, he finds the journals and responds to their contents. The danger of such a structure is that it provides excessively neat closure, that action so morally repugnant could become too satisfying aesthetically. This problem the author addresses by pushing the circularity of the novel beyond the comfort point: he adds, by way of a coda, part 4, in which Clegg is again investigating another victim—"another M," he exclaims—while at the same time denying the reality of his plan, exactly as he has done before. Closure suddenly becomes unsettling rather than reassuring, chilling in the recognition that Clegg will strike again, that he believes his mistake was aiming for a girl out of his own class. Readers will recognize in this ending the inevitability of Fowles's choice of point of view: that ending can only come from the character himself, since no other alternative can be nearly so frightening.

The point of view shifts in the novel reinforce the theme of Otherness, of mutual incomprehensibility, which will remain a major concern throughout his fiction. From *The Magus* through *A Maggot* the alien nature of the other sex infuriates, mystifies, goads, and inspires Fowles's protagonists. He takes the notion of one's muse, particularly the sexual element, seriously in a work such as *Mantissa,* but, even when the character is not a creative artist, his actions are spurred by a mysterious sexual Other. In *The Collector* such an idea is turned upside down by Clegg's refusal to try to understand Miranda's Otherness. Each male protagonist attempts to shape the female Other to his own preconceived notions; all but Clegg tend to be flexible enough, or to be forced by circumstances they cannot control, to recognize the inadequacy of their prejudgments. In part, as Mahmoud Salami asserts, Clegg cannot recognize that inadequacy because he does not see her: "Miranda is seen as the mirror: through her Clegg sees his 'self'; he only sees his reflection and forgets about her."[3] He has no outside force to act on him and no inner mechanism to check his excesses. He therefore becomes a kind of worst-case scenario of the male side of personality running amok: selfish, rapacious, suspicious, obsessed with control, sexually driven. That he embodies so many conflicts is a function of his inability to comprehend women. While driven by tremendous sexual desires, he is impotent at the thought of woman as sexual being. He can only understand females as idealized figures, as characters from fairy tales, or as fallen and therefore disgusting creatures. Miranda cannot reach him through argument, fits of pique, appeals to reason, or sexual allure. She is quite beyond his understanding and, as such, never becomes completely real for him. He sees her in light of his plans, his desires, his needs. After she dies he says that he can finally forgive her for all the things she did to him, completely failing to realize that none of those acts would have happened but for him and that depriving her of her liberty had an impact on her life as well as his.

At the same time, Miranda can understand him only slightly. In part, of course, that is a function of his madness, but it also has to do with her own preconceived ideas. She lacks sympathy for someone from the lower classes—real sympathy rather than the charitable urges that drive her to collect for Save the Children. She is unable to feel what it is like to be raised in a poor family, to have the kinds of pressures which affect those without money. Her exasperation with him in conversation is often a result of expecting him to behave as one of her social set might; when he cannot do that, when he is defensive and sullen rather than assertive and confident, she throws up her hands. The impossibility of their understanding each other stems from a number of dichotomies: male/female, lower class/upper class, poorly educated/well educated, mad/sane, with the last one turning their relationship into a most extreme instance of the problem of Otherness. Miranda attempts to unite these dual opposites, while for Ferdinand they remain hopelessly separated.[4] Numerous Fowlesian pairs will have their difficulties, and some may fail, but none is as deadly as this twosome.

The theme of Otherness is mixed up, in this novel as well as others, with that of power. *The Collector* is a study of power: its acquisition, its misuse, its corrupting influence, its effect on holder and victim alike. Clegg sees himself shut out of the any sort of earthly power, indeed sees himself as a victim of power. His army time reinforced his impression that people like him merely obey orders issued by people from Miranda's class, and his work experience has been the same, showing him that he is a very small cog in a very large governmental wheel. Equating money with power, he receives his football pool winnings and immediately begins to look for someone over whom to exercise power. He compares Miranda to creatures of delicacy and powerlessness, both because of traditional figurative language attaching to women and because it suits his purpose. At one point before the kidnapping she is "like a bird," while her hair is like "Burnet cocoons," and she herself is a rarity, like a "Pale Clouded Yellow" and still later a "Queen of Spain Fritillary." Such comparisons to things he already captures makes the kidnapping more acceptable to him. Even her death is foretold in his butterfly similes, when he says that watching her is like watching the imago appear but that then it must be killed. He is spared the act of murder only by allowing her to die of pneumonia. He always wants to see her as weak and needing protection, since protection is one traditionally sanctioned way of exercising male power over the female. This power relationship has a bearing on his impotence: he can masturbate while looking at dirty photographs, since the pictures give him complete control of the situation. William Palmer makes the connection among Clegg's obsessions: "Collecting, photography, and pornography—in Fowles's novel all three motifs represent different kinds of killing, and all are different types of perversion of the life-art relationship."[5] All three, in other words, reduce living creatures to objects, over which Clegg can assert his dominance. A living woman, however, even the prostitute, is a threat, since she endangers the completeness of his control.

Miranda threatens his control in various ways, yet in others she plays right into it. Her class itself constitutes a threat, as both her father's career as a doctor and what Clegg calls her mother's "la-di-da voice" symbolize. He cannot keep up with her in conversation or understand her ideas. Her aggressiveness is a very grave threat, as he shows when he objects to her using obscenity early in their relationship, and she responds by screaming obscenities at him, driving him out of the cellar. Later he loses all respect for her when she attempts to seduce him. It is not merely that she uses her sexuality but, rather, that she uses it aggressively which bothers him; "girls" should be passive, in his worldview. She quickly learns that she can get whatever she wants in the material line simply by ordering it from him and says of the situation that, aside from being deprived of her freedom,

"In everything else I am mistress." What she fails to see is that every demand she makes, every errand she causes him to run, simply ratifies his vision of her as dependent upon him. And she becomes so lonely that she actually hopes for him to come down and visit sometimes, again strengthening his position as the holder of power.

Miranda has some hang-ups of her own regarding male-female power. One is her vision of herself as a disciple, later as a wife, of the artist George Paston. She recalls her relationship with him, never an easy one, in which she takes his views as her own, accepts his judgments, defers to him in everything except his proposal of marriage, an offer about which she subsequently changes her mind. Bruce Woodcock notes a connection between Paston and Clegg through their desire to possess Miranda. In such a view Miranda has simply succumbed to the cruder version of male domination.[6] Paston, a forerunner of Henry Breasley in "The Ebony Tower," exercises what is for her acceptable male power. Indeed, Miranda is looking to be dominated by a man. She recalls telling her sister at one point that she could not go to bed with a man who was not at least her equal. This is more than just sexual snobbery; rather, it represents a sense that for a relationship to work the man must be at least as strong as the woman and that being stronger is all right for him. Her willingness to be dominated introduces a strong element of sadomasochism into her relationship with G.P., as Pamela Cooper has pointed out.[7] Her disgust with Clegg sometimes stems from his refusal to act strong, particularly in light of his role as her jailer. Her images mirror his in disquieting ways. She, too, associates herself with a fragile creature, as when she says her hope flutters against the glass of his killing bottle and realizes it is trapped (189). Against his use of *Secrets of the Gestapo,* she sees herself as Anne Frank, as the victim of an unspeakable misuse of power. For Fowles the Holocaust stands as the informing historical moment, revealing many things that are wrong with society in his time: insensitivity, cruelty, the urge to violence, the will to power. Nazis and their victims will appear frequently, and not always metaphorically, in his later work. In this case the mix is disastrous, since the Nazi in Clegg must find his Anne Frank in order to fulfill his role. Miranda's choice of a victim—rather than, say, a Resistance fighter—is telling, and possibly fatal.

The Nazi connection leads also to a growing strain of existentialism in Miranda's thinking. Many of those thinkers central to existentialism—Jean-Paul Sartre, Albert Camus, Simone de Beauvoir, Samuel Beckett—shared a background in the French Resistance, and one of the most illustrative works to come out of the movement, Eugène Ionesco's *Rhinoceros,* deals with a Nazi-like takeover. Miranda's experience of victimization and rebellion leads her to conclusions very similar to theirs. She begins to think there is no God or that God may exist but be completely indifferent to human fates, and finally she decides that "we have to live as if there is no God" (205). Her isolation leads to alienation, first from her captor, then from God, and eventually even from herself. Her efforts to escape eventually lead to despair and absurdity when she sends Clegg to London for the day and spends hours digging out a single stone, only to find a much larger stone behind it. In fact, the hopelessness of dealing with stones recalls Camus's *Myth of Sisyphus,* in which the mythic character is condemned forever to roll a stone up a hill.

THE COLLECTOR

Like Sisyphus, she initially gives up in her despair but then decides to persevere, declaring that she will survive, that in the face of overwhelming odds and insurmountable power she will nevertheless persist in her efforts. In the context of existentialist thought, whether she survives or not is less important than her resolve to continue the struggle. When everything else by which she has measured herself is stripped away and she has only herself to rely on, she still continues to battle with the forces that threaten to crush her, thereby achieving a measure of heroism, perhaps the only measure human beings can achieve in the Fowlesian world.

Notes

1. John Fowles, *The Collector* (Boston: Little, Brown, 1963) 10. Subsequent references will be noted parenthetically.

2. Carol M. Barnum, *The Fiction of John Fowles: A Myth for Our Time* (Greenwood, Fla.: Penkeville, 1988) 39–40.

3. Mahmoud Salami, *John Fowles's Fiction and the Poetics of Postmodernism* (Rutherford, N.J.: Fairleigh Dickinson UP, 1992) 61.

4. Salami 64.

5. William J. Palmer, *The Fiction of John Fowles: Tradition, Art, and the Loneliness of Selfhood* (Columbia: U of Missouri P, 1974) 40.

6. Bruce Woodcock, *Male Mythologies: John Fowles and Masculinity* (Totowa, N.J.: Barnes, 1984) 36.

7. Pamela Cooper, *The Fictions of John Fowles: Power, Creativity, Femininity* (Ottawa: U of Ottawa P, 1991) 41.

CHAPTER THREE

The Magus and the Existential Dilemma

Fowles's second published novel, his first in order of composition, *The Magus,* explores issues of existentialism within the setting of an exotic detective story. Like *The Collector,* the novel's conceit grows out of a tiny fragment of the author's experience, in the previous book his earlier butterfly collecting, in this case his time spent teaching on a Greek island. Also like the earlier book, this one diverges immediately from that germ of autobiographical detail. The story involves a young Oxford graduate, Nicholas Urfe, who finds himself at loose ends and accepts an appointment as an English teacher at a boys' school on a small Greek island. There he becomes involved with a mysterious Greek aristocrat, Maurice Conchis, and the equally Byzantine goings-on at his estate, Bourani.

Conchis stage-manages an elaborate series of bizarre encounters and performances that alternately titillate, befuddle, and infuriate his audience-victim, Nicholas. Because the novel is narrated by Nicholas, the reader is equally mystified by the actions of Conchis's "cast." As with the previous novel, Fowles displays his brilliance in manipulating point of view in this book. While Nicholas is an ingratiating and sympathetic narrator, he is as unreliable in his way as *The Collector*'s Clegg proves to be. Moreover, Nicholas is himself the audience for other narrators, each of them of dubious credibility, so that the narrative stacks levels of unreliability in dizzying profusion. Without being a programmatic follower of Sartre or Camus, Fowles raises not only the issues of modern existentialist philosophy but also the historical conditions that gave it rise. The basic set of conditions are laid out and, often, mentioned specifically. Nicholas presents himself as Man Alone—solitary, cut off, his parents dead, no siblings, lonely, an island unto himself. The Greek island on which he lands is symbolic of his own psychological state. He confronts the problems of ennui and inauthenticity and early on reaches a point of suicidal despair.

The "godgame," then, into which he stumbles offers him several reflections of his condition as well as potential solutions, or escape options, and analogues and sources in the German occupation and the Greek Resistance. The godgame is the novel's name for the series of performances and events staged by Conchis for Nicholas's benefit. (The word also appears in *The Aristos* as the heading for a section in which Fowles discusses the relationship of a god, if any, to human beings; his belief is that any deity would have to govern without seeming to govern, to exert its influence by vanishing.)[1] The role of Conchis, and of God, for Fowles is like that of the novelist vis-à-vis his fiction. Existentialism owes as much to living under Nazi occupation during World

War II, particularly in France, as it does to any philosophical antecedents. Many leading existentialists, including Camus and Beckett, were also active in the French Resistance. The Nazi context of the novel, with its implication of totalitarian control, leads to a meditation on freedom and its dangers. If freedom is absolute, if the gods have indeed absconded, then the individual is no longer moored by the traditional constraints. Instead, he or she must choose a personal path, determine right and wrong on a humanistic, not a theological, basis. The emphasis of the novel is on actions and their reasons, on what we do and why we do it. Fowles makes a distinction between development of the Self and mere selfishness as the basis for action. Ultimately, Nicholas needs to take control of his own life, to act responsibly for himself. Whether he succeeds or not is left largely to the reader, so that the novel becomes a Rorschach test of the reader's own attitudes, beliefs, and ideas.

At the beginning of the novel Nicholas Urfe, bored and alienated, begins an affair with an Australian woman, Alison Kelly. Nicholas's sexual history is extensive but shallow. Although he claims not to be a sexual predator, he "was a dozen girls away from virginity" when he graduated from Oxford; moreover, he claims to despise the sexual game, although he can explain his strategies for ensnaring women—using his loneliness as a trap—in considerable detail: "I had my loneliness, which, as every cad knows, is a deadly weapon with women. My 'technique' was to make a show of unpredictability, cynicism, and indifference. Then, like a conjurer with his white rabbit, I produced the solitary heart."[2] He displays his greatest disgust with women in regard to a senior master's daughter at Oxford, Janet, whose chief crime

THE MAGUS

was to fall seriously in love with Nicholas. Alison seems a perfect complement to this Lothario: rootless, virtually homeless, without romantic ties or illusions. She is an airline hostess living in a foreign country and tinged by that inferiority the imperialist Nicholas confers on everything colonial. When they meet she is involved in an unsatisfactory affair, which may or may not be pointed toward marriage. She promises, in other words, to be everything Janet was not, with the added attraction for Nicholas of providing him the chance of asserting predatory dominance by breaking up an existing relationship.

Yet Alison's fatalism regarding this new relationship masks a desperate need to be taken seriously, to be rescued from an unhealthy pattern of sexual liaisons, to be loved. Each time she deprecates or vilifies herself—"I'm going to be a stupid Australian slut forever," she says—she is asking, in vain, for contradiction. Because of his own ego-driven needs, Nicholas mistakes the mask for the reality, treating her as a disposable commodity rather than as a person whose concerns must be taken into account. He accepts her facade in order to maintain his own. His departure for the Greek island of Phraxos, then, is a welcome relief, coming at a time when Alison threatens to become serious about the relationship. From that safe distance he can alternately string her along, feeding his ego, and ignore her existence when it suits him to do so.

The Nicholas who arrives in Greece and becomes involved in the shadow play superintended by Maurice Conchis, then, is a thoroughgoing egoist whose sense of victory that Alison loved him more than he did her is more convincing than his professed self-revulsion at that elation. He also carries with him the preju-

UNDERSTANDING JOHN FOWLES

dices, largely literary, of northern Europe regarding the licentious South. For a century prior to this novel the Mediterranean has represented a loosening of restrictions, a holding in abeyance of the usual mores, from the myth as well as the work of Lord Byron, to whose death Nicholas alludes, to D. H. Lawrence's *Aaron's Rod,* Thomas Mann's *Death in Venice,* and Lawrence Durrell's *Alexandria Quartet,* the appearance of which preceded *The Magus* by just a handful of years. (Indeed, Nick shares a number of traits with Darley, the failed writer-hero of Durrell's tetralogy.) He actively hopes for a change in the moral climate, claiming that Greece makes English moral concepts "ridiculous." He is, in short, a nearly perfect audience for Conchis's drama.

Nicholas's readiness for change, his receptiveness to a new message is made the more complete by his own brand of existentialism. Clearly, he knows the poses that are appropriate to the existentialist mode. Alone, isolated among foreigners on an island, unable to communicate or connect with his fellow teachers, he is alienated from his work, from his fellow man, from women, and from himself. He perceives himself to be drifting aimlessly, completing his pose of self-ruin by catching syphilis in an Athens brothel. After nine months of such aimless drifting (and the time span's importance should not be discounted), in May he finally begins exploring Conchis's villa.

Fowles uses, rather than follows, existentialism. Certainly, he is fully aware of the precepts and practices of Albert Camus and Jean-Paul Sartre, as is his protagonist. Moreover, the novelist examines the issues raised by existentialism in his book-length collection of aphorisms and miniature essays, *The Aristos.* Spe-

cifically, Fowles is interested in questions of aloneness, alienation, absurdity, and meaning raised by Camus and Sartre. Yet
the artist in him also recognizes that such considerations can be
used as dodges and self-justifications by the whining Nicholas,
whose problems are more invented than organic. Alienation and
absurdity, for instance, can provide acceptable excuses for sloth.
Indeed, Nicholas seems afflicted chiefly with more traditional
problems: laziness, lust, refusal of responsibility, pride, self-
absorption, male ego. One hardly needs Camus to interpret such
a character. Rather, the terminology of modern existentialism
generally obscures rather than illuminates Nicholas's true motives. Alison actually has the truest expression of existentialist
thinking when she tells him that life lacks meaning "because we
don't believe in a life after death" (*Magus,* 36). It is one of many
opportunities she gives him early in the novel to contradict her,
to provide some kind of meaning, to offer love, but he fails to do so.

The novel avoids becoming an existentialist casebook by
exploiting the terms and concepts of the philosophy and by
attributing them to the conscious activity of the protagonist.
Fowles can thus grapple with the issues of modern existence
without being a programmatic follower of Camus.

One key point of departure from Continental existentialism is Fowles's belief in the importance of relationships for
providing meaning. While Camus in *The Plague* or Sartre in
Nausea stresses man as relentlessly alone, Fowles recognizes the
artificiality of that condition. Nicholas is an isolate on Phraxos,
to be sure, but he has had to flee a relationship in order to arrive
at that state. He wills himself to be alienated because it fits a
certain fashionable image of the *poète maudit,* the poet as

accursed outcast, which he would very much like to become. His inability to make a complete break with Alison and his immediate desire to form a relationship with Lily/Julie (she alternates between these two identities as her principal personas) point to the essential falseness of that pose. Even the last image of the novel, in which Nicholas and Alison find that the gods have absconded, leaving them alone, implies that they can only find meaning and self-definition through each other.

His loneliness and sexual longing while on Phraxos are sanctioned by his awareness of existentialist theory, and they make him highly receptive to his adventures with Conchis, a small, suntanned bald man of about sixty, noteworthy for his unusual eyes, which suggest something "not quite human." There will continue to be an element of questionable humanity in Nicholas's descriptions of the old man throughout the narrative. He is also notable for cryptic answers and sudden, unforeseeable shifts in conversation. Remarkably, Nicholas seems to be expected, although the two have never met. This is the first of many surprises and mysteries the younger man will encounter.

The ensuing meetings are equally perplexing for the young Englishman, partly because they fit into no clear pattern. Conchis is repeatedly contradictory, alternately gregarious and taciturn, forthcoming and elusive, while Nicholas, who by temperament and training expects consistency and clarity, desires simplicity over complexity. Conchis maintains a very extensive library yet burned all his novels before the last war, declaring that "the novel is no longer an art form" (98). He challenges the notion of wading through hundreds of pages of invented action for a handful of "little truths," declaring: "Words are for facts. Not fiction" (99).

Yet the godgame he apparently constructs answers very well to that description, an immense fabrication intended to reveal a few truths. He explains his complete opposition to war yet proposes an ideal society in which a game of chance resulting in ritual suicides for the losers takes its place. He claims to have saved the island during the Nazi occupation, yet his efforts made him appear to be a collaborator. Or perhaps he was a collaborator who now offers a self-justification.

Conchis reveals his method of narrative technique in his tale of his sweetheart, Lily Montgomery. Lily, a thoroughly conventional girl with all the prejudices and beliefs of her class, utterly rejects Conchis for his refusal to fight after he witnesses the horrors of Neuve Chappell; indeed, she represents his break with a British identity, or its break with him. She subsequently dies in the typhoid epidemic of 1916. His use of her story is exemplary: each element carries symbolic as well as particular meaning. The individual event or person is also representative of the archetype and may be subsumed by the archetype. Typically, Conchis underscores the key points of a narrative or document by directing a dramatic presentation. Lily, for instance, makes an appearance immediately after the story in which she is named— she, or rather someone (the woman Nicholas comes to know as Julie Holmes) in Lily's persona, simply walks through the room in which the two men sit—with Conchis declaring that this woman is neither Lily nor someone impersonating her. Before Nicholas can solve that conundrum, she passes from view. Earlier he has fallen asleep reading a seventeenth-century confessional pamphlet. When he awakes the characters described in it, a minister and the young girl he impregnates, appear before

him. While Nicholas cannot believe Conchis could have orches-
trated the scene—the randomness of his falling asleep near the
gully, having actors on hand who can seize the moment—he
nevertheless attests to its reality. For some reason, however, he
refuses to ask the direct and obvious questions about Conchis's
actions and motives in presenting such a scene. His typical
response to such a scene alternates between silence and coy
acknowledgment. It soon becomes apparent that, despite his
protestations that Conchis's machinations are "maddening,"
Nicholas is thoroughly taken in, wanting to see the next act, the
next plot turn.

His addiction hinges on several factors. One is the attrac-
tiveness of Lily/Julie and the resulting feelings of possessiveness
he develops. Another factor is the degree to which his masculine
ego is alternately inflated or punctured by events in the masque;
often he is as motivated by stung pride as by any success with
Julie Holmes (the guise in which she allows him to know her).
Still another is the need to follow the plot through to its conclusion. In this case plot works in both its literary and its conspira-
torial sense. At times Nicholas feels he is in the midst of a living
novel or play, while at others he senses himself the victim of a
conspiracy; in either case he needs to see some resolution of the
events, to put them into a comprehensible framework.

His need to understand grows out of his desire for power
and control: in every situation Nicholas seeks the high ground,
the commanding position from which he can dominate others. At
one point he decides to use Alison's impending visit as a
stratagem, to hold her at bay in Athens as a means of gaining the
upper hand. "I won either way," he thinks (207). Later, during
Conchis's absence, he pins Lily to the ground in a position highly

suggestive of rape and wrests a confession from her. Afterward he comments, "I ought to have realized earlier that a little force would do the trick" (213). He ends the following chapter with the most ungallant act of forcing a kiss on an unwilling partner. Still, he thinks, it meant more to Julie than to him.

His need for supremacy reveals itself most fully in his mistreatment of Alison during their long weekend together in Athens. He goes to Athens out of vague feelings of hostility and vengeance, although toward whom he cannot sort out. While Alison is not the presumed source of these feelings, she bears the brunt of his wrath. He notes at once her bruised quality, his phrase for her vulnerability, which both excites and repels him and which invariably brings out his predatory nature. He thinks of Alison in terms of how Julie—his version of "Julie"—would assess and dismiss her. He even lies to her about his syphilis, which he did indeed contract in an Athens brothel but of which he is now cured, using it as a pretext for not sleeping with her. Having Alison available for sex yet not having sex with her places him in a position of power: her willingness places her at the mercy of the dominating man, while she lacks the truth of his actions and motives.

Conchis, attuned to Nicholas's predatory nature, plays on it in creating the various explanations of Julie's presence on the island. The duped actress routine (which casts Nicholas as the rescuing knight) soon gives way to a fiction in which Julie is a mental patient under his care and in which he is himself a renowned Jungian psychiatrist. In this scenario Nicholas is the actor in the masque, the necessary outsider who provides Julie with contact with normal, young malehood outside the patient-caregiver relationship. Still later Julie and her sister, June, reveal themselves to be actresses not in a film but, rather, in a psycho-drama being presented for Nicholas's benefit; the twist on this seeming truth is that the masque has somehow run amok, that Conchis acts capriciously and without their knowledge, that he somehow abuses their services. There are even dark hints of sexual overtones in their relationships, a subtext that Fowles will make an overt element of the story in his novella, "The Ebony Tower."

The Conchis urtext, or the master story, which lies behind all these variations involves certain basic elements: a young, comparatively helpless woman whom the main character will find wildly attractive and sympathetic, a second young woman (a twin, no less) who is less appealing yet jointly involved, elements of mystery and even danger, the self-contained green world of romance, and the elderly puppeteer who controls all the actions of his underlings. The unstated extra feature, inevitably, is the young, handsome rescuer, which role Nicholas enthusiastically embraces. Indeed, while he often suspects he is being duped within the role, he never suspects that the role itself may be part of the subterfuge, that his "role" and his real part in the drama might not be consonant with each other. That lack of perspective, of course, sets up his downfall: he simply cannot envision the lack of character which makes a role of knight-errant preposterous for him. This story line, moreover, may also be seen as the Fowlesian urtext. The quest romances will follow similar paths throughout his career: "The Ebony Tower" (the most precise complement), *The French Lieutenant's Woman, Mantissa,* and *A Maggot* all involve similar elements. The constant features, naturally, are the enigmatic woman and the existential mystery, for these are male

THE MAGUS

quests and male mythologies.[3] It is through the mysterious Other that the Self begins to acquire understanding in Fowles's thought. Unlike Jean-Paul Sartre, Fowles does not believe that the Self can develop or heal in isolation but, rather, that it requires interaction with outsiders, with the Not-Self. Too much isolation, in Fowles's thinking, leads to narcissism and destructiveness. Since he writes chiefly from a male perspective, the Other has a strong sexual element: his masculine protagonists struggle to understand their female Others. While he has said that his female characters inspire him, they have never occupied the narrative center of consciousness in his novels. It may be that Fowles recognizes the falseness of a male novelist claiming such complete understanding of the feminine.

If Conchis's numerous versions of truth all have a highly composed quality, it is not merely that he is engaged in a fictive activity but also that his stories grow out of a master plot designed to appeal to male desire. Moreover, each is timed to supplant a recently exploded tale, providing a rapidly shifting succession of explanations that keep their prime audience disoriented. Indeed, some (like the madness tale) are patently unbelievable and seem to exist only to lend credence to a competing story.

Near the book's physical center, Nicholas has two sexual experiences, one with Alison and one with Julie. They point to his chief character deficiencies and mark a departure in the masque, for after this point the terms of the play cease to be personal and romantic, becoming more overtly moral and existential.

Despite his protestations of not loving her, Nicholas goes to Athens to see Alison. His behavior and thoughts surrounding this meeting demonstrate the powerful narcissistic and even autoerotic element in his nature, as everything seems to turn on him: his fantasies, his superiority, his control of the situation. He despises himself, or professes to, and claims, even while embracing her, that "it meant nothing, it must mean nothing" (265). His manner with her is unpromising, even hostile, yet he does not leave; while Alison is not his ideal, she nevertheless still holds an attraction. He forces her to take the initiative, and in the hut on Mount Parnassus she does. While they do not make love, his thoughts as they undress and caress reveal his need to tear her down. He compares her to a prostitute in her adeptness and her easy nakedness, never considering that he, among others, is responsible for that adeptness. Worse, he imagines the same scene with Julie, in which the experience is seen as "infinitely disturbing and infinitely more passionate" (269), not at all the accustomed and domesticated moment it is with Alison. A couple of pages later he remarks on Alison's "inability to live behind metaphor" (271) and wonders why he does not find that inability disgusting. When, a bit later, he confesses that he does not have syphilis and they make love, he claims that "sex would have been far wiser" (274), further stressing his contempt for Alison—and for his feelings for her. What Nicholas fails to recognize is that some charges he brings against Alison, while not true of her, *are* true of Julie, and that with others the comparison should favor the former rather than the latter. Julie's "performance" much more nearly resembles the prostitute's than does Alison's naturalness, that Julie's interest in him is feigned, Alison's real. It is only because of her relative mystery that Nicholas can attribute to Julie an infinite passion. What is more, it is precisely Julie's ability to hide behind metaphor, indeed behind deceit and role playing, that

THE MAGUS

he finds maddening. Yet because he wishes for the mysterious, the forbidden, he constructs an infinitely desirable "Julie" of his own. What is more, whereas he and Alison make love, Julie masturbates him (claiming she is having her period) while they are in the water, underscoring his autoerotic tendencies. Nicholas completely misses the point. Despite this manifestly one-sided eroticism, Nicholas's massive egoism allows him to decide again that "it meant more for her . . . it was the discovery, or rediscovery, of her own latent sexuality, through the satisfaction of mine" (376). His astonishing arrogance exceeds all known bounds: whereas previously he has seen the sex act as providing greater satisfaction for the woman, here such a notion is clearly out of the question, yet he still can claim to have done her a favor.

Slightly earlier, while he and Julie kiss in the chapel, he thinks of her "pent-up emotion, repressed need" (358), while forcing himself against her and asserting that she, not he, is "losing control." As ever with Nicholas, the need to be firmly in control of romantic or sexual relationships and to gain supremacy over his partner colors his thinking and his actions. He perceives her involvement in this intimacy as tangible evidence of her emotional trustworthiness. Moreover, he dissociates love and sex, despite Conchis's nonverbal warning: the older man leaves pornographic matter, including a book showing breasts not attached to bodies. Yet, as Katherine Tarbox points out, Nick repeatedly misses the point: "Fantasy . . . is essentially autoerotic, as is pornography, and both close him off from the reality of the exciting subject. The point of pornography is to allow one the impulse to make love to oneself. In this light it is easier to see why, in the revised edition, Fowles gives so much more weight to the 'erotic element,' and why he allows Nicholas to masturbate in front of us so many times: Nicholas is essentially a masturbatory personality."[4] His narcissism is tied to his more generally ego-centric view of the world: in sex, as in all other things, Nicholas is the center of the universe. Other people scarcely count, except as figures in his fantasy.

Fowles has brought Nicholas to his chief crisis point, to the very pinnacle of ego puffing. When Alison learns a bit about the godgame, she intuits (or perhaps she is already informed by Conchis) that there is another woman, throws Nicholas out, and the next morning is gone, leaving behind a letter that ends with the word *finished* repeated three times. In leaving, she eliminates his remaining link with his real-world past. Nick has denied Julie's importance to Alison, then denied to Julie that he has even seen Alison; he has had his way with both of them, rid himself of the old, familiar one, and presumably won the new, exotic one. Absolutely as full of himself as he can get, he is primed for the tearing down of that Self.

Conchis's first act of ego demolition, immediately after the bathing scene, is to introduce the great theme of his last story, this time allowing the dramatization to precede the narrative. Nicholas, on the way home, encounters a group of German soldiers, recalling the atrocities practiced by the Nazis during the war. He is captured and bound, and when they leave he must free himself with the aid of a dull knife they leave behind. Conchis follows by sending a note calling off further visits to Bourani, claiming they would be fruitless. Nicholas perceives some "obscure meta-physical lesson," although he prefers to see the act as wanton cruelty. Conchis then recants, allowing that message to come through Julie. Almost immediately thereafter word comes from Alison's roommate that Alison has killed herself. The newspaper clippings specifically mention an unhappy love affair, so that Nicholas is directly implicated. On the subsequent trip to Bourani, Nicholas is told the "truth" about his adventure: he is the audience-participant in an experiment in metatheater, a theater without proscenium, in which the barriers between actors and audience would be broken down. The point, Conchis claims, is for all parties to see through the drama, not to be taken in completely by the illusion but, rather, to doubt and think. This, he claims, is the *catastasis,* the period of falling action in a drama leading from the climax to the catastrophe. Nicholas, consumed by his need to comprehend and in some manner control the situation, fails to heed the warning: this is not an ending to the drama but, instead, a prelude to catastrophe. Major, possibly disastrous, events are forthcoming, yet he is unprepared.

Having issued this ignored warning, Conchis launches into his last, longest, and most important story: of German occupation, the torture of Resistance fighters, and an untenable choice forced on Conchis by the Germans. The guerrillas who had been captured had been horribly tortured—beaten, burned, their genitals cut off, their fingers crushed, their tongues ripped out. Conchis was forced to interrogate one of them. The only word the fighter utters is a screamed *Eleutheria,* meaning "freedom." The next day Conchis is given a choice: in order to save the lives of eighty villagers held as hostages, he must personally execute the prisoners. He complies, although of course the gun is unloaded. When the cruelty of the trick dawns on him, he joins the guerrillas, cries out *"Eleutheria"* and is shot with them and left for dead. A faked burial with an empty coffin follows as well as the suicide of the "good" Nazi, an Austrian named Anton. Although Conchis professes no courage, and although he gives himself over to be killed, he has no sympathy for Anton's passivity and suicide. Instead, he insists that man must struggle, take positions, be involved. The basics of the story—the Nazi brute, the nameless rebel, the ineffectual Anton—form for Conchis the only real story of Europe, implying by extension that they are the real story of modern humanity. The choices of freedom come down to those basic types: oppressor, doomed but valiant fighter, hand wringer. Nicholas feels himself identified with Anton, the weakling, the mild sensualist swept along by forces of greater moment.

Against his own version of freedom as hedonism and moral laxity, Nicholas realizes, Conchis has set a version of freedom which insists on personal responsibility and ethical accountability. Yes, we are free, Conchis seems to say, but freedom carries with it terrible burdens. If one is free to destroy another human being, one must also accept culpability for that destruction. Such a morally demanding freedom comes as a revelation to Nicholas, who responds, once alone, by thinking not of the pleasures of Julie but of the memory of Alison and of his "complicity" in her death (448). Yet even here he cannot fully accept responsibility. Instead, he generalizes the guilt that the living share for each death: not "I caused her suffering and her death" but, rather, "we cause their suffering and their deaths." Still, it is a start.

Nor is Conchis through with him. Rather, he continues the pattern of proffering and withdrawing Julie. On the next trip Nicholas finds the house shuttered and the occupants preparing for removal. When he and Julie go exploring a tunnel, she is suddenly whisked away and the tunnel cover slammed shut on him. As at nearly every stage of the adventure, there are symbolic implications, in this case of the trap of consciousness, of tunnel vision, of the dangers of psychological isolation. And, as at every other stage, Nicholas misses them. When next he receives information it is from June. She begins telling him another version, but he cuts her short with the story of Alison's suicide. At this apparent cue she drops her pretense and takes him to the village to Julie, previously claimed to be in Athens. June then announces that the experiment is off, telling him that Maurice is a psychiatrist and that the others are students and fellow professionals. It is in this guise that they will remain for their final appearances.

He does meet with Julie, telling her a partial truth about his weekend with Alison in Athens. The air seems to be cleared between them, at least to his satisfaction, and they make love during a heavy thunderstorm. Yet, even in the throes of postcoital bliss (he imagines they have regained Eden), he receives his greatest shock, finding himself suddenly kidnapped and drugged. After several days of drugged disorientation he is placed on trial before a panel of psychological investigators (who were previously players in the masque). The location, decor, and costumes are all heavily symbolic and mythological. The setting is a large underground cavern or cistern done in black and white with cabalistic emblems and motifs—a black cross, a huge red rose, a severed hand with first and fourth fingers extended. The thirteen figures attending the trial all wear bizarre costumes, led in by Herne the Hunter, the neolithic god with stag's head: an English witch, a man with a crocodile head, an African corn-doll, Anubis the jackal-headed, and so on, with Conchis as magus. The thirteenth figure wears a goat's head with black beard, white smock, and red gloves. After their astonishing entrance they unmask and claim professional identities, but the air of unreality lingers.

Having made themselves known as clinicians of various stripes, they turn their attention to an analysis of Nicholas's many character flaws and psychological insufficiencies. Distilled from its psychoanalytical jargon, the diatribe is intended to tell Nicholas in the most humiliating manner possible that he is an inadequate human specimen. Having played out the diagnosis, they throw another astonishing event at him. Julie/Lily is strapped to a flogging frame and Nicholas handed a cat-o'-nine-tails. Even here he cannot act spontaneously, as he would like to act, but is reduced to second-guessing Conchis and wanting to make a right choice in front of the students in attendance. He ultimately recognizes his choice as analogous to that which Conchis had to make during the war, carrying a great weight of responsibility with it, and he does not strike.

As part of a bizarre debriefing to an equally bizarre experiment, Nicholas is forced to watch a pornographic silent film involving Julie and Joe, her black nurse–colleague–lover (in his various guises), then to watch them make love in person. The reason, presumably, is to deprogram his infatuation with Julie, to allow him to get on with his life. The scene also has the effect of bringing Nicholas's racism, which has been present throughout, to the surface; tolerance is not among his virtues.

When, subsequently, truth shifts again and he is told that Conchis is dead, the reader at least is hardly surprised. Nicholas assumes the scene is a final joke on him and a warning not to pursue the detective game further, that all avenues will be blocked, or false. Again he misreads the message. On Conchis's grave is an arrangement of a white lily and red rose among inconspicuous white flowers. Nicholas reads the assertive blooms easily but ignores the less showy clusters, as has been his weakness through the start, and therein lies his mistake. The small white flowers are sweet alison (sweet alyssum). This fact he discovers only after he sees the supposedly deceased Alison, still very much alive, from his hotel window.

Once more Nicholas is spurred to pursue the quest for answers, yet even in his doggedness he shows that he has not learned Conchis's lessons. Following all known leads on Conchis's story, he finds them to be false, for the most part (587–94). He tracks down a Lily Montgomery, now Mme de Seitas, in Hertfordshire. The two are working at cross-purposes. Nicholas wishes to pursue a course of anger and recrimination, and he demands to find Alison. His impatience and brutishness reveal his failure to absorb the experience of Bourani. Rather than yielding to his acrimony, she makes him hear her version of reality, which emphasizes freedom and responsibility, love versus sex, true and false moralities. Maurice and the others are practicing a kind of living philosophical experiment, in which periodically they involve outsiders. Nicholas, meanwhile, can see only his hurt feelings, vowing never to contact her again, despite his need to see Alison. When he leaves, however, he finds that her facts all check out at Somerset House (the central British repository of births, deaths, and marriages) so that for the first time someone has given him objectively verifiable information. Still, he harbors resentment and impatience.

In fact, he cannot let go of his complex of resentment and hostility until he meets again with Mitford, his predecessor at the Greek school. Mitford is so prejudiced, so unpleasantly self-centered, so much the neo-Nazi, that Nicholas changes his attitudes nearly on the spot. He recants and contacts Mme de Seitas for another meeting. Before they can rendezvous he meets his successor, an American named John Briggs. Whereas only a few days earlier he would have done everything he could to dissuade Briggs from going, now he sends him on his way with good wishes and a smile. He seems to understand that every person's trial is different, that one cannot be warned off life.

His change of heart allows him to meet Mme de Seitas on a different emotional footing at the Victoria and Albert museum and later at a restaurant. She passes along two valuable pieces of information. Of immediate importance, she says, the godgame is over; whatever the purposes of Conchis and company, they are at an end, leaving Nicholas and Alison to their private fates. Nicholas does not know whether to believe this statement or not, although the presence of John Briggs in his world suggests it to be true. Second, he must wait for Alison, who is not a present or a trophy but who, instead, "must be paid for" (642).

Nor does Alison appear immediately. During the interim Nicholas strikes up a companionship with an odd, disheveled Scots girl named Jojo. During that relationship he comes to understand the supercommandment that Lily de Seitas has told him: "*Thou shalt not cause unnecessary pain*" (652). His lack of forthrightness has inflicted pain on Jojo, and he sees that it is another working out of his behavioral paradigm: selfishness causes pain to others. Presumably, he is prepared to meet Alison, yet more time passes before, on Halloween, he finds her, led there by his gruff, leftist landlady.

Nicholas may have been improved by his experiences, although how much one cannot be sure. His immediate reaction to Alison is suspicion and hostility, which may be a by-product of the godgame: he simply cannot believe it is over. Repeatedly, she sets him straight, "It's nothing to do with them now" (661). As they walk in Regent's Park, recriminations on both sides, she declares her intent to return to Australia, and, when he makes her choose between him and "them," the godgame he still believes is continuing, she chooses Australia again. As Carol Barnum notes, in this most Jungian of Fowles's novels, which makes free use of archetypal imagery and Self/Other, or anima/animus, dualities, the park is "a garden in the heart of London and in Jungian terms a mandala. The garden motif is important in another aspect, for it was in man's first garden, the Garden of Eden, that love was born, and by the symbolic act of returning to the Garden, love can be reborn."[5] The mandala, too, is a center point that humans yearn to find, or return to. When he walks away she calls him back, saying she came to see him because she thought he had changed. His response is to slap her, and only then does he realize that there are no watching eyes, that the gods have absconded, leaving the poor, puny humans to fend for themselves. The act of unthinking violence clears the air between them, and she can declare that she hates him yet also intimate that she still loves him. Nicholas declares that he now understands what love is and that he feels it for her.

The novel closes with an unresolvable Fowlesian frieze. The novel suddenly shifts into the present tense and the third person, as if the novelist has suddenly ripped the fabric of

Nicholas's narrative to reveal the artist's perspective behind it, although readers may also see the device as Nicholas bringing them up to the present moment:

> The bowed head, the buried face.
>
> She is silent, she will never speak, never forgive, never reach a hand, never leave this frozen present tense. All waits, suspended. Suspend the autumn trees, the autumn sky, anonymous people. A blackbird, poor fool, sings out of season from the willows by the lake. A flight of pigeons over the houses; fragments of freedom, hazard, an anagram made flesh. And somewhere the stinging smell of burning leaves. (668)

The passage leaves the action indeterminate: Will she forgive, will she leave, will Nicholas do anything constructive? No answers are forthcoming. Even the grammar of the passage is resolute in its refusal to help, as the verbs disappear and the sentences drift into fragmentary noun clauses. Readers may feel frustrated at this final narrative coyness, yet the answer to the relationship would mask another answer to a yet more important question: Can this person be saved? The real issue throughout has been existential. Can Nicholas take this meaningless existence he is living and invest it with essence, with meaning, with value? The results through the bulk of the novel have not been promising, yet there are signs in the late stages that moral and spiritual growth is possible. The closing epigraph, moreover, holds out further hope. It translates as: "Tomorrow he may love that has never loved; Tomorrow he may love who has loved." Of course, *may* is a large sticking point; nevertheless, the possibility exists. An easy yes-or-no answer to the Nicholas and Alison question would finally obscure the significance of his development. If Nicholas has not improved, then any romantic or interpersonal issues between them are mooted. Lily de Seitas is quite right in her implications that Alison would be wasting her time returning to the old Nicholas. Readers will inevitably come to a conclusion for themselves on the outcome of that final frieze, just as they will decide for themselves whether Nicholas has grown adequately from his experiences on Phraxos or if he is even capable of growth.

Like all of Fowles's novels, *The Magus* is relentlessly literary, abounding with allusions and borrowings. The author, while embracing the realistic tradition, is simultaneously postmodern, refusing to let readers settle into the illusion realism typically offers. The names are a case in point. Nicholas and Alison are the young lovers of Chaucer's "Miller's Tale"; in that bawdy fabliau young love has its day at the expense of the old cuckold, yet all the characters come in for their share of pain and humiliation. In this novel, of course, Nicholas must also undergo humiliation of a particularly sexual nature. While less painful than the branding of his namesake, he too is seized immediately after lovemaking with Julie, then drugged, held against his will, and put on trial. The surname Conchis perhaps recalls King Colchis, who in Greek mythology was Medea's father. Medea, deserted by Jason after helping him obtain the Golden Fleece, murders the other woman and her own children. There may be an analogous situation in Alison's revealing that she has had an abortion as well as in the mock revelation of her suicide, clearly a response of mythological dimension to thwarted love. That Conchis's messenger is named Hermes heightens the mythological element. Conchis's name also suggests the root word of *consciousness,* or *conscience,* especially in a book that has a great deal to say about both psychology and morality. It even embodies his refusal to fight after witnessing the horrors of war, for conscientious objectors were known more succinctly as "conshies" or "conchies." Is he trying to bring Nicholas to consciousness or to moral responsibility? Perhaps a bit of both. The remainder of the names in the novel *are* literary creations. Julie and June each has numerous roles they play, as the Edwardian sisters Lily and Rose Montgomery, as "Julie" and "June" Holmes in their other main guise, and as psychiatrist Dr. Vanessa Maxwell and her costume-designing sister, Margaret Maxwell. Each of the names is suggestive of a type of woman at a given historical period and, as such, equally suspect. Even their common names, suggesting the summer months as they do (and Northrop Frye calls romance the mythos of summer, the mode of literature which grows out of the season),[6] strike the reader as less than plausible.

Certainly, the novel draws heavily on the elements of romance, from the Gothicism of *The Turn of the Screw* and *Great Expectations* to the more pastoral romance of Henri Alain-Fournier's *Le Grand Meaulnes* (translated in English, significantly, as *The Lost Domain*). As Mahmoud Salami points out, "the quest for a mysterious lost land and its beautiful, unknown girl" is central to each novel, as indeed it remains in much of Fowles's work.[7] Just as the romance often turns on a quest, so it frequently involves issues of illusion and reality, as in the James and Dickens works. All three works, but especially Alain-Fournier's, lie behind *The Magus.*

There is, however, a more prominent source. While the names of the young lovers derive from Chaucer, the context is overtly Shakespearean, drawing theme and substance from *The*

Tempest. Conchis invokes Prospero very early in his discussions with Nicholas, and from then on the play is never far from the reader's awareness. Fowles borrows from other Shakespearean plays, notably in Nick's sense of himself as Iago and in the use of faked death from *Much Ado about Nothing* or *Twelfth Night,* but the central locus of references is clearly to *The Tempest.* Nicholas himself mentions parallels between his situation and that of Ferdinand, while Julie calls attention to patterns from *The Tempest* later on in the novel. The main parallels have to do with the lonely island setting, with Conchis as magician or stage manager, like Prospero, and with Nicholas as the young suitor who is repeatedly thwarted and tested as he acts out a controlled psychodrama. He assumes, of course, that the casting leaves Julie in the role of Miranda, never considering that parallel may be inexact and that it may be Alison of whose love he must prove himself worthy. Indeed, Julie may be more the Ariel figure, leading Nicholas where her Prospero would have him led; that Conchis "frees" the sisters from the script late in the drama emphasizes such a reading. Shakespeare's late plays are his most problematic, not fitting neatly into established literary categories of tragedy or comedy. Yet when Prospero releases the others from his spell, sinking his book "some fathoms deep," the plot resolves itself in comfortable ways, with the promised marriage of Ferdinand and Miranda, the exposing of culprits, and the reconciliation of feuding parties.

The ending of Fowles's novel, on the other hand, remains problematic in characteristically postmodern fashion; the resolution refuses to come, and the closing remains unsettled. What, after all, does happen in that closing frieze? Will Nicholas and Alison reconcile, or are the wounds too deep for healing? In *The*

French Lieutenant's Woman Fowles will proffer a Dickensian double ending; here he employs even greater subtlety, creating a moment that contains multiple, exclusive possibilities. His sources, too, tend toward indeterminacy or a lack of clear resolution, from the two endings Dickens wrote for *Great Expectations* to the governess's questionable narrative closure in James's novella. While it is true that, as Patricia Waugh says, "ostentatious use of literary and mythic allusion reinforces the notion of fictionality, and the reader's awareness of the construction of alternative worlds,"[8] such intertextual strategies also attempt to sanction the more difficult-to-handle elements, such as indeterminacy, of the novel. Throughout his work he maintains an uneasy relationship to closure in narrative, and his novels and stories generally end with unanswered questions, enigmas, hanging resolutions. Just as life in his novels is like literature, his literature is like life, where unfinished business abounds.

The Magus can be seen as an allegory of the act of reading, in which readers find themselves pulled and manipulated in numerous ways, not all of them pleasant, yet they are unable to resist its attractions. At the end they may or may not have learned anything that will make them better human beings and may not be certain about what the text wanted to teach them. The narrative itself remains largely unchanged by their passing through it, just as Conchis's godgame has survived Leverrier, Mitford, and now Nicholas. Like Charles Smithson in *The French Lieutenant's Woman,* Nicholas functions as the first reader of the events of the novel, performing the same acts on events which readers must perform on the text itself. As Salami notes, part of his unreliability as narrator stems from his activity as reader and critic of the already unreliable narratives of Conchis, Julie, and others.[9] When Nicholas realizes that the godgame is over, it is only over for him, as the novel is only "over" for the individual reader, while the novel itself is never really completed so long as there is another reader, or even potential reader. Even the apparent changes in Conchis's "text" which tailor it specifically to Nicholas may be only reflections of his own egocentric involvement, just as each reader of *The Magus* finds a slightly different novel, colored by the sensitivities and inclinations of that reader. The problematics of meaning, in such a transaction, lie as much within the "receiver" as within the "sender" of the message. That Fowles's novels are routinely ambiguous, unsettled, problematic, requires a great deal of the reader in terms of investment of personality and values, just as the action of the novels typically requires a similar huge investment from the protagonists. Those requirements will become more pronounced and overt in his next novel.

Notes

1. John Fowles, *The Aristos* (Boston: Little, Brown, 1970) 18–20. Subsequent references will be noted parenthetically.

2. Fowles, *The Magus: A Revised Version* (Boston: Little, Brown, 1978). Subsequent references to this edition will be noted parenthetically.

3. See especially Bruce Woodcock, *Male Mythologies: John Fowles and Masculinity* (Totowa, N.J.: Barnes, 1984), for a discussion of Fowles's use of the male-oriented myths of romance.

UNDERSTANDING JOHN FOWLES

4. Katherine Tarbox, *The Art of John Fowles* (Athens: U of Georgia P, 1988) 24.

5. Carol M. Barnum, *The Fiction of John Fowles: A Myth for Our Times* (Greenwood, Fla.: Penkeville, 1988) 29.

6. Northrop Frye, *The Anatomy of Criticism* (Princeton: Princeton UP, 1957) 186.

7. Mahmoud Salami, *John Fowles's Fiction and the Poetics of Postmodernism* (Rutherford, N.J.: Fairleigh Dickinson UP, 1992) 79–81.

8. Patricia Waugh, *Metafiction: The Theory and Practice of Self-Conscious Fiction* (London: Routledge, 1984) 113.

9. Salami 77. See also Waugh 111–13.

CHAPTER FOUR

The French Lieutenant's Woman: Postmodern Victorian

When *The French Lieutenant's Woman* appeared in 1969 it caused an immediate stir in the reading public and the critical community. Twentieth-century fiction to that point had spent much of its energy attempting to escape from the legacy of the Victorian novel, yet here was John Fowles not merely borrowing from but mimicking that form. In the ensuing decades others would follow his lead, from Fay Weldon to Charles Palliser to Robertson Davies to Susan Sontag to A. S. Byatt, ranging from parody to earnest imitation. Yet Fowles's novel is neither a spoof nor a copy of a Victorian novel; rather, it is an exploitation of the form. In this borrowing of form, the novel shows itself to be solidly in the postmodernist camp. Beginning with Jorge Luis Borges and Vladimir Nabokov on through John Barth and Italo Calvino, writers since World War II have used elements of other genres and other centuries to construct their fiction. Fowles, however, is among the first to return to an earlier form of fiction as a way of constructing his novel.

Throughout the book the emphasis is on contrast between the two centuries. First is the issue of subject matter. The story is set in 1867, a pivotal year in Victorian England, with the publication of Marx's *Das Capital.* The characters are all resolutely Victorian, and Fowles keeps them in character. Yet the import of the story lies outside their milieu and within ours. The first question here is: Why should the author elect to tell a Victorian story in order to make points about life in his own time? In order to answer that question one must look at the dominant philosophies, sexual attitudes, and artistic movements of the time.

Fowles makes much of utilitarianism, of the work of John Stuart Mill and Jeremy Bentham, but chiefly in order to balance its problems against those of existentialism. Similarly, he plays High Victorian, Pre-Raphaelite, and Decadent Art off against one another, complete with two competing images of the author himself. And, finally, the central question of the story regards nineteenth-century attitudes toward love, marriage, and sexuality and their twentieth-century counterparts. How we respond to the novel, therefore, depends in large measure on how we respond to these Victorian attitudes and the people who hold them. Why, for example, do readers not find Ernestina attractive? Is Sarah an emissary from modernity, from the beginnings of the twentieth century?

Within this framework of ideas Fowles engages in an interplay of forms, combining Victorian conventions, parody, pastiche, essay, and elements of the Gothic in a way that is completely postmodern. The tale calls attention to this formal oddity through the use of numerous devices: anachronistic refer-

THE FRENCH LIEUTENANT'S WOMAN

ences, epigraphs from sociological studies of Victorian England, the heightened awareness of the historical moment, knowing histories of the characters' subsequent lives, indeed the twin endings themselves.[1] The author's obviously contemporary interest in narrative indeterminacy undercuts expectations of certainty and resolution embodied in the Victorian structure. Fowles is not Hardy or Dickens, however much he may admire their accomplishments, and the aesthetic assumptions under which they operate can never be his.

In his well-known essay "Notes on an Unfinished Novel" Fowles says that the novel grew out of a single image: "A woman stands at the end of a deserted quay and stares out to sea. . . . The woman had no face, no particular degree of sexuality. But she was Victorian; and since I always saw her in the same static long shot, with her back turned, she represented a reproach on the Victorian Age. An outcast."[2] *The French Lieutenant's Woman* is in a sense merely an attempt to complete that image, to give life to that lonely figure, to find her story. And to an extent he is doomed to failure; Sarah Woodruff remains always out of reach, distant, unknowable, the least fully realized character in the novel, metaphorically out on the quay with her back turned, a reproach to male novelists, perhaps, as well as to her age. Yet it is precisely this mystery that drives the novel, that brings to life other characters and pushes them to action.

If that static, feminine image starts the author on his path, it also launches the action. In the opening scene Charles Smithson and Ernestina Freeman are walking along the quay on a blustery day in Lyme Regis, when they come upon the figure. Ernestina sketches in the woman's story—ruined and abandoned by the

French lieutenant, now a bit mad, known as Tragedy by the gentry, as the French lieutenant's whore by the working class (the title of the book uses Ernestina's bowdlerized version). When Charles tries to entice Tragedy away from the end of the Cobb, as the quay is known, he is rebuffed by a glance that cuts through him, full of sorrow and aloofness. Instantly, although he denies and makes light of its importance, Charles is caught up in that glance. Discerning readers will notice something more: while Charles cannot know it, being a creature of the narrative, he is also caught in the shift of narrative modes. He and Ernestina, his fiancée, travel in the realm of light realism, what one could follow Yeats in calling the "casual comedy." There is nothing casual or comic about Sarah. She, like the setting she chooses for herself, comes straight out of the dark Romantics—tragic, stormy, attached to the deeper impulses of the Self, ignoring social convention. Ernestina, inspired by the sunnier moods of Dickens, is "young, beautiful, and good," in his phraseology, if a bit silly and cloying.[3] Sarah is a female Heathcliff. Charles must inevitably find her more fascinating. Even the narrative surrounding her is more charged, more interesting, than that dealing with Ernestina, so that readers will also be drawn to Sarah. Although Ernestina accuses Charles of lacking romance, Fowles notes that he inclines toward a Byronic stance, that he has "all the Byronic ennui with neither of the Byronic outlets: genius and adultery."[4] His readiness, therefore, to be swept into a Romantic novel is established early on.

Sarah, naturally, is unaware of her special credentials. Since she is a character within the narrative rather than a participant in its creation, she can only see herself in terms of victimiza-

THE FRENCH LIEUTENANT'S WOMAN

tion, not of artistic mode. In the externals of her story she most resembles Hardy's Tess: pushed out of her class by a ne'er-do-well father, she is socially stranded and sexually exploited, so that ultimately she has no home and no support structure. Sarah is too well educated to marry into her own class but too poor to marry up. Apparently suffering from melancholia (what is now called depression), she accepts a position in Mrs. Poulteney's house, the least appropriate situation for her in the town. Mrs. Poulteney allows Fowles to indulge his considerable comic skills. She is narrow-minded, bigoted, hypocritical, tyrannical, obese, peremptory. While she wishes to perform charity by taking Sarah in, she screens her as if hiring an employee. She wishes to save some poor sinner, but not one who has actually sinned. Whether Sarah accepts to further punish herself, as depressives often do, or because it ratifies her view of the world, we do not know. Her two chief reasons are that the house affords a view of Lyme Bay, to which she seems addicted, and that she has been reduced to penury, with only seven pence to her name.

Sarah is presented as a figure of considerable sympathy. Despite her lack of conventional beauty, the narrative says, her mix of understanding and emotion would have made her either a saint or a king's mistress in an earlier day. She practices a form of passive resistance, even when succumbing to orders, which her benefactress finds maddening. She is unorthodox in her views and manners; in an age in which orthodoxy is prized above all else, her inability or refusal to conform makes her a refreshing literary creation. She repeatedly contradicts her betters, either in terms of station or gender, and this frankness sets her aside from the clinging Ernestina, who invariably yields (or pretends to yield) to Charles's views. To Charles it is the combination of mystery, isolation, victimization, and assertiveness which makes Sarah irresistible.

Modern readers may be particularly attracted to Sarah because of her existentialist suffering. Although she cannot recognize them (being born a century too early), she exhibits the symptoms of existentialism as delineated by Sartre and Camus. She is alienated from herself, from God, and from society. She has her moments of absurdist recognition and suicidal despair. Her life is without essential meaning, and ultimately she must take charge of her life and invest it with meaning, must create her being as she goes. Like Sisyphus, she has been condemned to a certain life, in her case not rolling a rock up a hill but, instead, living singly in a society that values only wedlock for women, and, after wallowing in misery through the first half of the novel (to the point of contemplating suicide), she chooses the heroic option of embracing that condition and making something positive of it. Unlike Nicholas Urfe, who revels in the poses of existentialism, Sarah is genuinely trapped in an existentialist situation without the knowledge or skills that would provide a guide out of that trap. Her struggle to find her own way out, along with Charles's fascinated observation, forms a large part of the novel's plot.

Charles's own grappling with existentialist realities serves as the other major focus. Charles moves from a comfortably conformist role in society, despite his protestations of being his own man, to being an outsider who must confront his own lack of authenticity. While he believes himself to be a Byronic loner and skeptic in the beginning of the novel—and his tweaking of the middle class by following Darwin is his chief supporting evidence—Charles is very much a product of his time and class. He lives on a private income, with expectations of further inheritance of money and title when his uncle dies. He is a nonproductive member of society, and even his fashionable scientific interests are dilettantish, pursued without system or rigor. When he breaks his engagement with Ernestina he is forced outside society, both by Mr. Freeman's threats of exposure and by his own growing sense of alienation, largely brought on by his inability to find Sarah. In "Notes on an Unfinished Novel" Fowles asserts that the Victorian age was profoundly, if unwittingly, existentialist. Certainly, in its fiction, Dickens, Eliot, and Hardy in particular, the age embraced the same concerns as Sartre and Camus and company. Pip's struggle to become a "gentleman" in *Great Expectations* shares many elements with existentialism—that meaning and value must come from within, for instance. Both Hardy's Tess and Jude are tormented by alienation from God and man. The chief difference between their situations and Charles's is that his creator possesses an adequate terminology to discuss his plight.

That plight is central to the novel, for, despite the title and the occasional authorial references to Sarah as "the protagonist," Charles stands as the main figure in the novel. Feminists have rightly noted that Fowles typically concerns himself with male protagonists and male dilemmas, that female characters play secondary roles, and this novel is no exception. This twist, of course, reflects the age; it may be termed the Victorian era, but it is dominated primarily by such men as Lyell and Darwin, Tennyson and Browning, Marx and Mill, Disraeli and Gladstone,

Dickens and Thackeray and Hardy. Even the Pre-Raphaelites, who figure in the novel tangentially, with their fetish of sacred and mythic womanhood, were totally dominated by men— William Morris, Dante Gabriel Rossetti, Edward Burne-Jones. Women were figures of great interest and mystery for the Pre-Raphaelites—in fact, almost the only fit subject for painting—but chiefly because of their Otherness, their foreignness, rather than because of any great understanding on the part of the artists. So, too, with *The French Lieutenant's Woman:* Charles is brought to consciousness through the agency of a woman he admires but does not understand. That woman appears to be miles ahead of him in her own coming into being, yet her presentation in the novel is sufficiently limited that such an appearance may be illusory.

As the novel opens, Charles is the typical wealthy Victorian bachelor on the verge of marriage. Considerably older than his fiancée, he treats her condescendingly, while she behaves like a coquettish and sometimes petulant schoolgirl to his suave Oxford man. He drifts along in what the narrative calls "tranquil boredom" (16), playing his role as young aristocrat. He playfully teases his valet, Sam Farrow, who responds with cockney indignation, both of them conforming carefully to preset roles. His relation with Ernestina is chaste and slightly distant; neither of them ever says anything meaningful or revealing, and even their proposal scene is sealed with a ludicrously asexual kiss. He has followed Ernestina from London to Lyme Regis in an age-old courting ritual of hide-and-seek: if he will follow, then he must be serious. It is, naturally, a game only the wealthy can afford to play.

It is as happily betrothed strollers that they come upon Sarah Woodruff standing at the end of the Cobb, where she rebuffs and attracts Charles with her gaze. He subsequently encounters her on one of his fossil-finding expeditions to the Undercliff, the steep, eroded cliff beyond Ware Commons. When he discovers Sarah sleeping his first impulse is to turn away and not disturb her. But then, prompted partly by the memory of a sleeping prostitute in a Paris hotel, he continues to watch, another of Fowles's voyeurs. Like his counterparts Nicholas Urfe in *The Magus* and David Williams in "The Ebony Tower," he is paralyzed at the brink of action, torn between sexual desire and fear at the risks desire carries with it. And, like them, his voyeurism represents the larger struggle between the impulses of engagement and isolation, of active involvement in life and passive observation of it. She wakes, however, and catches him watching her, and again their gazes lock, with a kind of inevitability: "Charles did not know it, but in those brief poised seconds above the waiting sea, in that luminous evening silence broken only by the waves' quiet wash, the whole Victorian Age was lost. And I do not mean he had taken the wrong path" (62–63). Readers will instantly recognize the rhetoric of sexual seduction in this passage, with its breathless pause, its lapping of waves—long the cinematic cliché for sexual climax—and in the overstatement of an age being lost. Charles has most certainly started down a different kind of wrong path.

Yet on another level Fowles means exactly what he says about the Victorian age being lost. What is at stake in the novel is nothing less than a way of life. The existing power structure of Victorian society is present throughout the novel, from the odious Mrs. Poulteney and her henchwoman, the misnamed Mrs. Fairley, to the self-made success Mr. Freeman, to Dr. Grogan and his adherence to the best medical opinions of the day, to the Methodist dairyman, to the pert yet orthodox Ernestina. Charles is in danger, as the novel progresses, of becoming merely another pillar of the Victorian establishment. He occasionally displays the humorlessness that passes for moral rectitude, or he wears the mask of "Alarmed Propriety" in dealing with Sarah, or he takes his class privilege too much for granted. The peril is both personal and cultural, since falling into the habits of one's society leads to an ossification of both the individual and the society.

The dichotomy Fowles sets up is between the structures of society, which he feels are inherently fascistic in their efforts to inflict conformity, and the self, which is inherently revolutionary in its insistence on its individuality, in its refusal to conform:

> All states and societies are incipently fascist. They strive to be unipolar, to make others conform. The true antidote to fascism is therefore existentialism; not socialism.[5]

> Existentialism is the revolt of the individual against all those systems of thought, theories of psychology, and social and political pressures that attempt to rob him of his individuality. (*Aristos,* 122)

One of the attractions of the Victorian society as subject matter for Fowles is its strong impulse toward unipolarism, toward unthinking conformity. The presence of Sarah, then, as one who refuses to conform is not a mere affront to that society but an active threat, since assertion of the Self thwarts totalitarian impulses. The novelist, however, is interested less in this historical insight than in its modern parallel. The history of the twentieth century has been one of constant assaults on individuals by a host of totalitarian schemes, among which Hitler is the representative

THE FRENCH LIEUTENANT'S WOMAN

figure. Fowles makes this point clear in his repeated analogies and references in the book to the Nazis and those who fought against them. Yet Fowles writes *The French Lieutenant's Woman* in the midst of a decade that stands as one of the premier assertions of selfhood in the history of any century, and he knows that the battle between Self and society is eternal and constant and not yet lost. When Charles loses his way as he gazes into Sarah's eyes, he begins to lose his conformity, begins to see the possibilities of the radical Self.

Those possibilities reside, apparently, in her eyes, for each time they meet Charles is aware of her eyes. When next they meet he notices her eyes are "abnormally large, as if able to see more and suffer more" (74). On this occasion she begs him to tell no one that he has seen her on the Undercliff, thereby implicating his own eyes in her secret. She is forbidden by Mrs. Poulteney, who has what Fowles calls a Puritan fear of nature, from visiting Ware Commons and the Undercliff. During an audience at Mrs. Poulteney's, to which Charles has been dragged by Mrs. Tranter and Ernestina, Sarah and Charles exchange a secret look unnoticed by the others, who have averted their eyes. Sarah's eyes are far-seeing, unlike those of the myopic Ernestina, as she gazes out to sea. She often seems to look through Charles, or past him. Her stare is almost otherworldly; that world, of course, is the twentieth century. If the shortsighted Ernestina represents the present as weighted down by the received ideas of the past (she unpleasantly echoes Mrs. Poulteney during the interview), then Sarah's fixed stare represents the pull of the future.

These two women, then, represent as well as produce the dilemma Charles must struggle with: Will he remain a creature of his own time or move into the future? Ernestina, with her love of bright colors, her adherence to the latest fashions, and her rejection of some of the more outmoded Victorian strictures, stands as a thoroughly "modern" young woman, vintage 1867. Yet her modernity is very much of her time; that is to say, she is as up-to-date as a girl could manage to be while remaining firmly in her own era. Her activities, her speech, her clothing, her taste, are all firmly informed by the culture that contains her. In no measure does she challenge or reject the basic demands and assumptions of Victorian society. Marriage to her would mean ossification for Charles: his tendencies toward stiffness, toward propriety, toward conventionality, would overcome his countervailing impulses toward flexibility, independent thought, and individual action.

Sarah, on the other hand, embodies values more closely associated with the twentieth century, and her influence, her ability to mesmerize Charles, has a great deal to do with the strangeness of that future time. Curiously, Sarah's plight is entirely Victorian in nature: the marital impasse she faces, the ostracism because of her scarlet past, her occupation as governess, and the lack of career paths available to her are all nineteenth-century impositions on her liberty and autonomy. Yet she maintains that autonomy, insists on that liberty, in the face of overwhelming social forces. Even her appearance suggests modernity. Fowles describes her as lacking anything like conventional prettiness yet having a beauty that the High Victorian era could not recognize—full lips, dark eyebrows, dense and wavy hair, and, of course, those astonishingly frank eyes. Modern readers can recognize the features as those of Elizabeth Siddal, Jane Morris, and Alexa Wilding, the favorite models of the Pre-Raphaelites, and the directness as that of our own century.

Her look is frequently described as naked, as the narrator emphasizes the eroticism connected with her and also the freedom from conventionally "clothed" responses. This tendency also manifests itself with literal clothing. Repeatedly, Charles encounters Sarah in various degrees of shedding garments: her bonnet, her cloak, and, in the fateful scene in Endicott's Family Hotel in Exeter, her day clothes entirely. He finds her seated in her room in her nightgown, all of the ordinary restraining garments removed. Significantly, when he meets her after their separation she is dressed in a simple shirt and skirt, not at all in the trussed and layered manner of Victorian fashion. The simplicity of her ensemble approximates that of the century to come, in which female modes of dress would become simpler and, ultimately, more masculine.

Sarah's final garments underscore her tendency to usurp what her society views as masculine prerogatives. She often contradicts Charles or else speaks out of turn or too frankly for his comfort. Indeed, she scarcely takes his feelings into account except to manipulate them (or so it seems to him), never to defer to them. She acts toward him, in other words, very much as a woman might act toward a man in the 1960s, not in the 1860s. When the narrator describes her mix of "emotion and understanding," he does so in terms of the past, saying those qualities would have made her "a saint or an emperor's mistress" in an earlier day, yet he cannot say what she might have been in our own day. Nevertheless, readers will recognize in her the beginnings of the liberated modern woman: she thinks her own thoughts, shapes her own identity (the French lieutenant's whore is, after all, her creation), and ultimately pursues her own destiny. Her one sop to her own time is her deferential posture, which she assumes when commanded or corrected, yet even that she typically undercuts with a look or a statement that suggest a less than total submissiveness.

Charles, naturally, sees the choice not between centuries but, rather, between women. His decision is not any easier for that, since he knows so very little of women; indeed, Charles's mystification throughout the novel is largely a product of the Otherness of women. Like many of Fowles's heroes, he has grown up and lived in an all-male environment. His parents are deceased, and his one elder influence is his lifelong bachelor uncle, Sir Robert. The public school and Oxford experience, of course, would have been entirely male in Charles's youth, and among his confederates at his club the only contact with women is with prostitutes and entertainers, two types shaped by men's fantasies of women, rather than by the genuine articles. His chief contact with females has been on the basis of superior power. His class, his masculinity, his educational status, all confer on him the upper hand in contact with women. With such women he is glib and self-assured. Even Ernestina, his intended, is a marked inferior on the basis of age, gender, and class (her father is nouveau riche, a commoner to Charles's aristocrat). Their conversations are shallow, if sometimes sincere; Charles routinely assumes superiority, while Ernestina, who can be quite petulant, consistently defers to him in important matters. When she does contradict him, during their meeting with the abominable Mrs. Poulteney, it is on the subject of the unreliability of domestic servants, an area of supposed female expertise. Even then she realizes her transgression and apologizes immediately when they are alone. What Charles lacks, then, is any knowledge of a woman as a complete person, someone with views, feelings, and a history that are hers alone, rather than a concoction brewed up to please the dominant male power structure.

Because of his lack of information, Sarah poses a significant problem of interpretation for Charles. He becomes the readers' representative within the novel, trying to decode and understand Sarah, just as the readers on the "outside" of the text must try to interpret each character. Some critics, like Mahmoud Salami, have seen her as a creator of texts, of stories and parables that teach.[6] It is perhaps more accurate, however, to understand Sarah herself as a text to be read. Not only her narratives but her sheer presence require active reading by Charles, as well as by others in the novel. Such a view of the novel can be quite fruitful, since it gives readers a means of understanding the different Sarahs presented to different audiences. The general public of Lyme Regis is presented with a very simple text: Sarah as fallen woman, ruined by a wicked foreign seaman, sensual and unrepentant. To Dr. Grogan she is another text, a case study of an unbalanced woman. In fact, he turns her literally into a text by presenting Charles with the medical documents pertaining to a similar case revolving around another young French officer, a Lieutenant La Roncière, falsely charged with raping the young daughter of his commanding officer. Grogan attempts to explain Sarah's behavior in terms of Marie, the girl in the case study.

To Charles, however, Sarah presents another, very different, text: constantly shifting, sometimes contradictory, unpredictable, unfinished. Each time they meet she produces some new bit of information, some new slant on her personality. She is occasionally the wanton, more commonly the damsel in distress (a role made more plausible by living in the house of Mrs. Poulteney, a reasonable facsimile of a wicked stepmother), borderline madwoman, solitary, villain, victim, lover, betrayer. She places herself in his path by going repeatedly to Ware Commons and the Undercliff, where she knows he goes to pursue his fossil collecting, then asks to be left alone. Making sure he sees her, she asks him to tell no one that he has seen her, thereby implicating him in her secret. She seeks out his help but does so clandestinely, appealing both to his gallantry and his ego (he is special, he alone can help her). She reveals progressively more of her story, yet it is not always consistent, and the main point, as he discovers, is untrue. When Charles finally goes to Endicott's Family Hotel and they make love, he finds to his shock that she is a virgin. She has never made love to the French lieutenant. His reading of her moves from victim of romantic impulses to victim of a narrow-minded society to manipulative, selfish marriage wrecker. That last image settles in more firmly when, having broken his engagement and returned to Exeter, he discovers that she has vanished.

Yet even then he is not satisfied with his interpretation, like a reader who finds a novel missing its last, most critical chapter. He waits for two years while his agents search for her, partly out of love and partly out of an anxiety of uncertainty: he wants to know why she has done what she has done. Unlike ordinary readers, Charles gets his chance to question this extraordinary author. If the text of Sarah is radically unstable, it is sufficiently provoking to spur him to action. The search for her authentic text is complicated by Charles's construction of a fantasy text, onto which he projects his desires. That alternative text, as Salami notes, is a "masculine narrative" in which Sarah is "a mystery, a dangerous Eve, and a contradictory subject."[7] Charles can never understand, or "read," Sarah until he learns to accept her feminine narrative without bending it to the will of his masculine desires and prejudices.

Throughout Charles's search for the "real" Sarah, readers are confronted with an analogous search for the real novel. *The French Lieutenant's Woman* has become famous for its twin endings, yet they stand as merely the final instance of narrative gamesmanship in a long catalog of slippery practices. The most obvious example is the use of the nineteenth-century novel form itself, for, while Fowles makes faithful use of the elements of that form, he never pretends to be writing a Victorian novel. Carefully assembling the elements of such a work—the story of Charles and Sarah could easily be by Eliot or Hardy—he repeatedly violates the illusion of reality by intrusive comments and stratagems. From the outset he insists on the differences between the nineteenth century and the twentieth, and he compares characters and situations to literary examples from the major Victorian novels. He compares the valet Sam Farrow, for instance, to Dickens's Sam Weller and, at another point, asks if he is a Uriah Heep. No Victorian, and certainly not one of the great realists, would risk damaging the presentation of their illusion with such an artful reference. Elsewhere he compares gentlemen of Charles's day with those of our own, again reminding readers of the artifice of his creation. His crowning moment, though, is chapter 13. Having asked, in closing the previous chapter, who Sarah is and what drives her, he opens this new installment by saying frankly:

"I do not know. This story I am telling is all imagination. These characters I create never existed outside my own mind" (80). He goes on to discuss the conventions of Victorian storytelling, including the omniscient, godlike narrator. He says, however, that that mode can never be his own, since he lives in the age of Alain Robbe-Grillet, the driving force behind the New Novel, and Roland Barthes, the French structuralist and narrative theorist.

His assertions put him firmly and consciously in the postmodernist camp, exploring its concerns, especially those of self-conscious narrative, distrust of realism, exploitation of previous forms, and narrative indeterminacy or unreliability. The effect of these concerns is to thwart the readers' desire for *story,* even while fulfilling it. If a writer believes that realism is essentially false, that it is an effect produced by a series of devices designed to trick the reader, among them the pretense that the writer is not making it all up, then his response may be, like Fowles's, to call attention to the artifice of his enterprise. The self-consciousness he displays in chapter 13 is characteristic: he reminds the reader that none of this is literally true or that it is true only in imaginative terms. In fact, Fowles chooses chapter 13 very carefully, on the basis of two well-known antecedents. One is Samuel Taylor Coleridge's *Biographia Literaria,* the first thoroughgoing treatment of literary theory in English. In his chapter 13 Coleridge discusses, in what is probably the most famous passage in the work, the distinction between fancy and imagination. George Eliot's *Adam Bede* includes, in chapter 17, "In Which the Story Pauses a Little," a discussion of her theory of novel writing and her views on imitating reality in her works. Fowles, then, conflates these two preoccupations into his profession of artifice, reminding readers that they should not confuse

THE FRENCH LIEUTENANT'S WOMAN

the action of the novel with real life and inviting their complicity in pursuing this view of the novel. What he finally argues for is the aesthetic consistency of fiction: it need not imitate any external reality so long as it provides an aesthetically satisfying whole.

And if the novel's wholeness is internal—that is, the narrative is true only to its own principles, not to any outside "standard"—then the readers' perceptions of those principles, and that truth, is as important as anything imposed on the narrative by the author. What he begins to argue for in chapter 13 is the aesthetic autonomy—the self-containedness—of the novel as well as the primacy of imagination in its creation. Aesthetic autonomy, however, is a function not only of the writer's creation but also of the readers' perception: How do readers view and understand the wholeness, the integrity, of the novel? The novel is a transaction between the two parties, then: the creator and the audience. For instance, the narrator is unable to fill in all the details of Sarah's motivations and internal life, so readers must surmise for themselves what drives her. The rightness of their interpretation is determined not by the narrator stepping in with a "final" version of Sarah but, rather, by how completely each reader's interpretation fits the facts of the narrative and explains her actions to that reader's satisfaction. There are numerous possible Sarahs in the novel, and different readers will undoubtedly reach different conclusions about her, many of them equally valid in the context of the novel.

That context is itself highly plastic, since Fowles extends the logic of chapter 13 out into the remainder of the novel, and especially into the twin endings. Since readers are participants in the creation of meaning in the novel, giving them a choice of endings completes their involvement. Partly, this stratagem is a canny salute to the Victorian novel, in which public sentiment often did dictate the course of fiction. Readers wrote to Thackeray, for instance, suggesting that two characters should wind up married to each other, and, in the most famous incident, Edward Bulwer-Lytton dissuaded Dickens from using his original, "unhappy" ending for *Great Expectations* in favor of the ending in which Pip and Estella are reunited. The reason: the reading public would not like an unhappy ending. The two endings also reflect the process novels, especially novels dealing with romantic involvements, go through in readers' minds. "I didn't like that ending," every literature teacher has heard. "Those two should (not) have gotten married." Readers mentally rewrite endings to suit themselves, to make the novel come out right according to their tastes, envisioning the novel they would have written had they been the novelist. Fowles simply insists that they are the novelists, that they determine the final course of events through their choice of endings. One of the criticisms sometimes leveled at the novel concerns the number: Why two endings? Why not a dozen or a hundred? In practice, though, the Victorian model he follows admits of only two endings. Either the principals get together, or they do not. Moreover, two opposed endings act as a kind of litmus test for readers, suggesting that, where romance is concerned, there are two kinds of reader and asking each one, "Which kind are you?"

Fowles's use of postmodern gamesmanship is, however, hardly a textbook exercise. He undertakes it in a spirit of great fun. His comments are arch and knowing, his asides are sly, his allusions are diverting, and he brings himself into the novel in two quite different, but equally amusing, guises. The first is as a large,

THE FRENCH LIEUTENANT'S WOMAN

solid man who is "not quite a gentleman," perhaps a successful, bullying Low Church lay preacher who engages in cheap rhetoric. Having had his bit of fun, Fowles reveals the traveler in Charles's railway compartment as his narrative alter ego and confesses his difficulty in knowing what to do with his hero. Later, after the first ending, the reunion version, has played itself out, Fowles again appears, this time in a much more garish and socially aggressive form. Sporting a stylishly trimmed beard, malachite-headed cane, and rather too much jewelry, he looks like he has deserted the pulpit for grand opera and been much more successful there. The chief reason for his appearance is to wind his watch back fifteen minutes, thereby allowing the scene between Sarah and Charles to play itself out again to a different conclusion. Yet the delight with which Fowles transforms his image from the railway compartment shows that the description, far from being a pretense, is a reward in its own right. The theoretical implications of his appearance and the self-portrait justify the scene that contains them as much as it justifies their appearance.

Readers sometimes express dismay or outright hostility at the self-referential games Fowles engages in, since they see that part of the work as an interruption of the novel. Such a view rests on the somewhat naive notion that the story *is* the novel, and the author himself is partly to blame. To be sure, Fowles believes in story, in the old-fashioned pleasures of narrative, and he delivers those pleasures in abundance. He is so good as a storyteller, in fact, that readers may be caught up to the extent that they believe the story to be, like its Victorian forebears, the entirety of the novel. One cannot, however, in good conscience write an 1867 novel in 1967; as Fowles repeatedly notes, too much has changed—in our worldview, in our understanding of literature, in our society, in our theology—to continue with narrative in the manner of James or Hardy. The "interruptions," then, are the novel, or, rather, the interplay between the narrative and its interruptions constitute the business of the novel. Fowles wants to do more than simply bring the story of Charles and Sarah to a satisfying resolution: he wants to bring readers' involvement with the story of Charles and Sarah to a satisfying resolution as well. To do that he must make readers aware of how the narrative works on them and how they work on the narrative. For instance, chapter 13 is a response to a cliff-hanger question. By pausing the story's progress to assert his inability to control all aspects of the novel, Fowles calls attention to the device of the cliff-hanger chapter ending. It is a trick novelists engage in, one that keeps readers turning pages or, in the Victorian originals, that kept them waiting for the next month when new pages became available. Postmodernist writers feel they can no longer engage in those tricks without simultaneously pointing them out as tricks. Novelist and critic William Gass declares in *Habitations of the Word* that readers are no longer naive, that they know the devices and ploys that novelists have used, and therefore novelists after Joyce and Nabokov and Borges can no longer write as if they were working in the eighteenth or nineteenth centuries.[8]

What makes these departures interesting, ultimately, is their sense of play. Part of the legacy of realism and naturalism has been a high seriousness about the business of literature, yet it is well to recall that both writers and readers have traditionally turned to fiction as entertainment, as diversion, as play. Even the

THE FRENCH LIEUTENANT'S WOMAN

Greek tragedies, with their strong element of religious teaching, operate primarily as entertainments. For Fowles, as for other postmodernists, the theoretical or didactic purposes assume a secondary role to creating a work that someone will want to read. The strong element of play, the lightness of tone in the narrative interruptions, can be misread as a lack of seriousness or a lack of commitment to the story. Rather, such playfulness should be seen as a total commitment to engaging readers' attention at all levels: not merely the emotional level, at which the Victorian novel chiefly operated, but also the intellectual and aesthetic levels. Fowles's play, then, is not an abdication of artistic responsibility but, rather, a function of that responsibility: he seeks to make us care deeply about his characters and to recognize both why we care (largely a function of the novelist's involvement) and why we care the way we do (a function of the readers' involvement).

Readers may wish for a naive or simple interaction with the text; Fowles insists on a sophisticated, complex interaction, giving us the product while also involving us in the process of fictional creation. Postmodernist texts that are completely given over to revealing the process, to exploring theoretical implications while scrapping story altogether, find scant reader interest. Fowles, however, avoids this trap with his commitment to traditional narrative. At the same time, had he written a conventional historical novel in the manner of the Victorians, *The French Lieutenant's Woman* would likely have sunk from view long since. That it endures and continues to sell many copies year after year, that it persists as a favorite among literature students, speaks to the success of his experiment.

Notes

1. Barry Olshen, *John Fowles* (New York: Frederick Ungar, 1978).

2. John Fowles, "Notes on an Unfinished Novel," in *Afterwords: Novelists on Their Novels,* ed. Thomas McCormack (New York: Harper, 1969) 60–61. Subsequent references to this article will be noted parenthetically.

3. See William J. Palmer, *The Fiction of John Fowles: Tradition, Art, and the Loneliness of Selfhood* (Columbia: U of Missouri P, 1974) 23–25, for a fuller discussion of Dickensian sources in the novel.

4. Fowles, *The French Lieutenant's Woman* (Boston: Little, Brown, 1969) 19. Subsequent references will be to this edition and will be noted parenthetically.

5. Fowles, *The Aristos* (Boston: Little, Brown, 1970) 121. Subsequent references will be noted parenthetically.

6. Mahmoud Salami, *John Fowles's Fiction and the Poetics of Postmodernism* (Rutherford, N.J.: Fairleigh Dickinson UP, 1992) 128.

7. Salami 123.

8. William H. Gass, *Habitations of the Word* (New York: Simon & Schuster, 1985) 156.

CHAPTER FIVE

The Ebony Tower and *Mantissa:*
Subjectivity and Truth

While Fowles has made his critical name primarily as a writer of extended fictions, he has departed from that path on two occasions, publishing shorter works that attempt to work out critical or epistemological problems. *The Ebony Tower,* Fowles's only collection of shorter fiction, considers many of the same problems of sexual and interpersonal relations as well as formal demands that have dominated the earlier fiction, adding to them the more narrowly artistic concerns of inspiration, authenticity, subjectivity, and honesty. His protagonists are involved in constructing reality, whether through art (the title novella), critical narrative ("Poor Koko"), or police detective work. They encounter other characters who would either inspire or thwart those efforts. In *Mantissa* he deals directly with the struggle between writer and muse, an issue he has flirted with in much of his earlier writing. In this case, too, the limitations of subjective perception inform the action of the novel. Because the books are so similar in concerns, one may think of them in tandem, as experiments wherein the novelist investigates matters that trouble him but to which he cannot devote massive novels.

The Ebony Tower

The novella "The Ebony Tower" will be quite familiar in structure and substance to readers of *The Magus.* A young Englishman travels to a foreign, isolated locale, where he meets an obstreperous-yet-wise old man, who is accompanied by two young women, one of whom becomes a love interest for the young man. Through a series of encounters that are as symbolic as realistic, the young man receives the opportunity for growth and development, which nevertheless he fails to achieve. The surface details differ, as does the element of crisis and resolution, yet the basic stories are closely related. David Williams, an artist and writer, has gone to Brittany to interview Henry Breasley, an expatriate British artist, for a book on Breasley's work. There is a built-in antipathy between the two, since Williams is an abstract expressionist and Breasley is an abstraction-hating traditionalist whose main sources are distinctly medieval and Renaissance. Breasley, the very model of the artist-as-old-rake, has with him two young women, whom he calls the Mouse (real name Diana) and the Freak (Anne). The Mouse acts as amanuensis, drafter, and muse; indeed, the old man explains to David that her nickname is a corruption of muse, with the *o* a symbolic representation of the vulva. For Breasley inspiration is inseparable from sex, whereas for David Williams art is entirely cerebral and sexless. The Freak plays out the role of post-1960s libertine, providing the openly sexual element in the artistic masque as well as companionship for Diana.

At the same time the three residents play these roles, however, they act out another set. Diana is not only the muse but the imprisoned princess as well. She is an aspiring artist, a former student at the prestigious Royal College of Art, but she will not become an artist in her own right until she escapes from the isolation of Breasley's world. In this context Breasley's gruffness and impossible behavior cast him as the ogre, yet he has less to do with Diana's "imprisonment" than does the outside world, which has given her little reason to join it. This scenario casts David as the knight-errant who has come to rescue the princess; yet, while the role holds great attraction for him, he may be miscast. That such an interpretation is put on the situation and events by the characters is made clear throughout the novella: there are references to Chrétien de Troyes and Marie de France, to Robin Hood and the myth of the "old green England," and to unspecified princes and knights-errant.

From the outset the text announces that David Williams has stumbled into another world. The estate is called Coëtminais—literally, "the wood of the monks," the sacred wood—and stands as a self-contained refuge from modernity, complete with sham fortification in the form of a rickety gate with a rusty, nonfunctional lock. The rituals of Coët are essentially manorial, the rhythms traditional rather than modern. Breasley's longtime muse is Mathilde (yet another Fowlesian *M* name for books and muses), the subject of his postwar nudes and now his cook. Her husband, who spent those postwar years in prison for murder, acts as groundskeeper and handyman, and the couple appears exactly as elderly retainers of the manor. Mathilde is the only person with whom Breasley never loses his temper; Diana describes his attitude toward her as that of a vicar with his favorite parishioner.

The comparison points up the tendency of the atmosphere to veer into the overtly religious, the sacred wood being monastic as well as magical. The girls, Diana especially, use the estate as a cloistered, "safe" environment; Diana has come after a disastrous love affair in the outside world and now fanatically guards her privacy. Even Rennes, the nearby town, has become too much for her with its traffic, its population, and, particularly, its men. She recounts a tale of meeting two young men in town, then panicking that they would wish to come out to Coët, even as she realizes that she is being silly—"As if I was a virgin or something. A nun."[1] She has become a nun, after her own fashion, a nun of art rather than of the church. Denying herself the conventional pleasures of sexuality and companionship, she has instead become wedded to the institution that is Henry Breasley. Indeed, she has considered, is still considering, his literal offer of marriage. Such an eventuality would prove calamitous to her own art and even her life, the narrative makes clear: the artist cannot retreat into another's fantasy but, instead, must engage the world on one's own terms. It is this possibility from which David Williams must save her. Retreat into the cloister is one of the perils facing the heroine of romance, the other being destruction by villainy; here they amount to largely the same thing.

Of course, this being Fowlesian territory, the cloistered atmosphere carries with it a distinctly sexual element. The Mouse shows up at dinner in a high-necked Edwardian dress but without a stitch on underneath. Breasley's talk about the girls is shot through with sex, as is their own talk, especially the Freak's. When they all stroll off for a picnic by the lake, Anne and Diana make a considerable show of stripping down to swim nude and, with the old man's assistance, entice David to join them. Traditionally, of course, the questing knight is confronted with distractions and temptations, with sex or false romance featuring as prominently as self-doubt or indecisiveness. The two come together in David's case. On the last night of his visit he and Diana are alone (through the Freak's rather obvious stage management), and the means by which he can help save her, clearly, is through sex. David finds himself in the position of either being unfaithful to his wife, Beth, or being false to himself and thereby failing Diana's need. If this dilemma resembles that in Marie de France's medieval romance *Eliduc,* on which it is based, the resolution looks much more like Fowles: David contrives to fail in both directions. He pulls back from Diana's need when she expresses it, not out of marital loyalty but, rather, out of fear of censure (Fowles's antipathy toward the "suburban" dimensions of David's psyche is typical) and a fear of risking any part of himself. David, readers have already come to understand, must always play safe. Then, after Diana has had to accept his rejection, so that the act would be nothing more than sex, he proposes that they could still go to bed, thereby sacrificing any claim to fidelity. She refuses him, and so he remains faithful to Beth despite himself. There can be no sense of triumph or virtue on any level for David Williams.

Clearly, the moral universe Williams faces is murkier than the one confronting Eliduc. Whereas Marie's hero could perform his act of contrition by building an abbey to which both women in his life could retire, that outcome is precisely the one Diana needs to avoid. Eliduc wins the heart of the princess while serving her father; David can win the princess, but that outcome will prove devastating to Breasley, while leaving her behind will destroy her. In no sense can he have both Diana and Beth; the role of modern women (and they both have talents and career aspirations of their own to prove the point) will not lead to such a tidy resolution. Yet he also lacks the boldness, the courage in its original sense, the heart, to bring about a positive outcome. Modern through and through, David seeks acceptance rather than honor, is driven by approval rather than passion. The medieval quester embodied the aspirations of his society; the Fowlesian postmodern quester embodies the shortcomings of his. "The Ebony Tower," then, stands as an ironic reworking of *Eliduc,* as Carol M. Barnum has pointed out, with the images and situations presented but reversed or undercut.[2] David thinks, "Would any decent prince have refused [Diana]?" yet refuse her he does. The ultimate, usually unstated, goal of the quest is self-knowledge and growth, and this is true of the ironic quest as well. Yet David's self-knowledge will not help him, for he finds himself unable to grow; he comes up against his limitations and cannot break through.

All of the romance elements, of course, have artistic implications, since all the principals are themselves artists. Breasley is a throwback to the past; he claims not to know the names of modern artists or to know them disparagingly. Picasso becomes "Pick-arsehole" and then "Pick-bum." The art of Coët is similarly old-fashioned: the chief piece is Breasley's immense *Moon-Hunt,* recalling Paolo Uccello's painting *Night Hunt* (1465).

THE EBONY TOWER AND *MANTISSA*

Breasley derides the abstract expressionism practiced by David and his contemporaries as overly cerebral and bloodless. He calls it unsexed art, which the Mouse translates as meaning that "abstraction represents a flight from human and social responsibility" (39), although Breasley's own version is more colorful, involving blunt references to bodily parts and functions. He has no use for artists who play safe, and he suspects David is such a one. David, as if to prove the point, has thought of his own work as "going well on walls," as being domestically acceptable. Breasley is the novella's version of Conchis from *The Magus,* the wise old man who acts as mentor, if cryptically, to nonplussed youth. Yet neither his teachings or Diana's peril can save David Williams from himself. The implications are clear: he is destined to be a second-rater, incapable of the ferocity, the passion, and the depth of feeling required of the great artist. These qualities, so manifest in Breasley (whatever his deficiencies as a social animal), elude David.

Breasley is, in his idiosyncratic way, a seeker of truth. Whereas David desires chiefly not to offend—he is forever looking for the diplomatic way to make a statement, for answers that will gain approval, for the consensus view—Breasley says exactly what he thinks, without consideration for the views of the feelings of others. David constantly feels tested in his exchanges with the old artist, yet he never considers the possibility of Breasley's statements being taken at face value. If one is at odds with the artistic standards of one's time, the novella asks, must one accommodate one's opinions, or one's art, to those standards? Robertson Davies asks a very similar question in *What's Bred in the Bone,* in which his protagonist paints two anonymous

UNDERSTANDING JOHN FOWLES

masterpieces in the style of the sixteenth century then gives up original artwork. Significantly, both Fowles and Davies are masters of the big novel, throwbacks to fiction of the Victorian greats, yet both are also steeped in contemporary fictional theory and practice. In *The Aristos* Fowles calls the Renaissance "the last period in which content was at least conceded equal importance" to style.[3] Breasley's art, then, like that of Davies's Francis Cornish, recalls the Renaissance's insistence on content, on communal rather than private meaning, on shared iconography. In being so radically *individual,* Breasley ironically insists on an art that is less private, less a product of romanticism. He embraces truth, what the Mouse calls "human fact" (43), with the ferocity and certainty of Dante consigning enemies to Hell.

The problems of truth and knowledge are addressed in the following stories of the volume. In "Poor Koko" Fowles presents a narrator who is largely consumed by solipsism and who discovers the dangers of encountering the world. The protagonist-narrator, a writer, has taken up residence in a cottage owned by friends in order to work in solitude on his biography of the nineteenth-century novelist and essayist Thomas Love Peacock—a decidedly minor literary figure. Physically puny and myopic, he uses his intellect and his vocabulary as weapons of intimidation. On his first night in the cottage he is awakened by a burglar, who imprisons him, first in bed without his glasses and then in a chair restrained by sticky tape. After collecting his take, the burglar unaccountably destroys the writer's manuscript, notes, working text of Peacock, and typewriter. He follows this act by incongruously giving the writer the "thumbs-up" gesture the writer associates with mercy. As most readers note, "Poor

THE EBONY TOWER AND *MANTISSA*

Koko" is the only Fowles work in which the conflict does not involve gender as a major issue. Because these two characters are male, the terms of their antagonism are necessarily placed elsewhere, chiefly on age and class. Indeed, the older man calls attention to this fact by his choice of title: *Koko,* he tells his readers, is a Japanese word for "correct filial behavior, for the proper attitude of son to father" (176).

The battleground for this conflict is language: throughout their encounter the two engage in a war of words, with communication and books figuring prominently in their conversation. While the burglar engages in a lengthy monologue on his craft, on social inequality, on Marx, the narrator critiques his use of language. Certain linguistic tics catch his attention: the use of *right* at the end of sentences, calling the older man "dad" and the omnipresent "man." The narrator is most comfortable dealing with the world through the filter of criticism, whereas the burglar believes in language as praxis. For example, the narrator chooses to understand the other's use of *man* as a desperate attempt to speak frankly as "a kind of recognition, perhaps even a kind of terror of all that did separate us. It may not be too farfetched to say that what I failed to hear . . . was a tacit cry for help" (173). Of course, it is too farfetched to say such a thing. He has just acknowledged the near universal usage of *man* among the young, yet he goes on to assert that it must have special resonance in his own case.

Most hilarious, however, is his analysis of the use of *right.* The burglar appends the word to the end of a great many phrases in the way an American might use "you know" or a Canadian "eh." This does not, however, stop the narrator from deconstructing the usage as a special instance: "It means in effect, *I am not at all sure that I am right.* It can, of course, be said aggressively: 'Don't you dare say I am wrong!' But the thing it cannot mean is self-certainty. It is fundamentally expressive of doubt and fear, of so to speak hopeless *parole* in search of lost *langue.* The underlying mistrust is of language itself" (173–74). He goes on to see this supposed linguistic deprivation as "the true underprivilege." In so doing, he reveals anew his prejudices, almost all of which grow out of class and privilege: the young man's "working-class" language is not the narrator's "middle-class," educated language, so it must perforce be inferior. The narrator's language is meant to be elitist and exclusive; his books are for the literary few. That he can refer to his work *The Dwarf in Literature* as a potboiler suggests the degree of his removal from common readers, much less nonreaders. He suspects the young man of having a better mind than his language suggests, that the young man may even be playing him for a fool, yet he largely dismisses such possibilities. The narrator, in other words, can see everything except his own privileged position, and that exception blinds him completely.

The young man, on the other hand, approaches language as being within the realm of practical action. His accusations against the older man take the form of failing to communicate on a meaningful plane: "You're just saying words, man" (151), and "Man, your trouble is you don't listen hard enough" (162). That is to say, the writer fails at both ends of the speech transaction. His disdain prevents him from treating the younger man as a genuine audience, and he spouts a good deal of high-flown but ultimately irrelevant or useless rhetoric. Similarly, the narrator is indeed guilty of only hearing the younger man through his own highly subjective filter—of not taking the burglar's words as statements of his position. The young man uses his language to explain why he steals from houses, why he attacks property, why he would never "do" a museum. His reasons are sufficiently clear, if inelegantly phrased by the narrator's standards. There is even a sort of poetic compression to his speech. When he binds the writer to the chair he also gags him, which is both part of the villain's ritual and a withholding of speech. It is only after the writer is bound that the burglar performs his ultimate speech act, burning the manuscript. This final act represents the young man's assertion of power—physical power taking on an aspect of linguistic power. He has entered into writing the Peacock book by causing it to be written again; the writer can bring no word of the restored book into being without finding himself reminded of this destruction.

The conflict between their attitudes toward language and the immolation of the Peacock study remind readers of the metafictional dimension of the story. This is a tale in which the basic material of fiction, language, is called into question. Before the writer is gagged the two discuss the possibility of his writing the young man's story or of the young man writing it himself. The narrator likes to believe his fate was sealed when he refused to write about the burglar, but in fact he was already being tied up at that point. Moreover, although they each say they will not write about the young man, he is being written about. He's a stickler for telling it "how it really is" (160), while the older man goes in for analysis, for imposing his view on his material. The young man may, as the writer maintains, want the word *magic* used on himself, but he wants a certain level of mimesis as well as a certain fluency; it is unlikely that the story at hand would meet with his approval.

There is a tendency among critics to see the narrator as one who has been brought from blindness to whole sight through his encounter with the burglar.[4] The evidence, however, is not encouraging. He has certainly gained some measure of understanding over his previous state, and he does acknowledge that he was guilty of not hearing at the time. Yet his hearing in the present is little better. He understands the young man only in terms of his own prejudices and presuppositions, and he attempts to shape the narrative according to his own elitist impulses, as his choice of title suggests (even his own friends fail to understand it). His failure to grasp completely the opportunity for change fits into the larger pattern of Fowlesian problematic. Nicholas Urfe has the chance but fails in *The Magus,* David Williams certainly fails in the title novella of this collection, as do the characters in "The Cloud." Even Charles Smithson's growth is open to debate, depending on which ending of *The French Lieutenant's Woman* one inclines toward. To leap too quickly at positive resolutions simply because they are available constitutes a danger for the reader of Fowles.

Resolutions become even more elusive in the final two stories of the collection, "The Enigma" and "The Cloud." The former plays off readerly expectations concerning the mystery genre. Yet just as "Poor Koko" undermines the thriller form it employs, so "The Enigma" simultaneously exploits and subverts the conventions of the detective story. And, like *The French Lieutenant's Woman,* the story emphasizes its fictionality, its made-up quality. When John Marcus Fielding suddenly disappears without a trace, Detective Mike Jennings is called upon to solve the case. The story has all the elements of a conventional mystery: the important person who vanishes and leaves political and social as well as familial questions unanswered, the detective who needs to solve the case for personal as well as professional reasons, the upper-class family that resists investigation and must be handled with great sensitivity and tact, the loyal-to-the-death secretary of the great man, the beautiful young woman who may or may not know something significant. Fielding is the generic upper-class modern man: conservative M.P., board member for City companies, country squire, lawyer, honorary master of foxhounds; indeed, it may be just this generic quality that he wishes to escape, if disappearance or suicide was his intent. In the hands of Agatha Christie or P. D. James the story would proceed according to plan: the detective, Hercule Poirot or Adam Dalgliesh, would pursue facts in the face of resistance and mystification, and in the end, through either brilliant insight (Poirot) or dogged determination (Dalgliesh), he would unmask the villain. As a member of the official force, a special branch sergeant, Jennings follows more closely in the procedural detective model of James, with a major exception: while he can run down leads and eliminate some possibilities, he ultimately cannot solve the case. Characters—the rebellious son, the loyal secretary, the publicity-shy wife, colleagues and rivals—are forthcoming or not (in line with their own interests) to varying degrees with facts and opinions.

Jennings's efforts, however, lead nowhere until he interviews the son's girlfriend, Isobel Dodgson. Like the others, Isobel can (or will) provide no substantial evidence to help solve the case. The difference is that she enters into a discussion of the imaginative possibilities of the case, tracing out possible scenarios for what happened to Fielding after he left his briefcase in the British museum reading room. Isobel offers Jennings a course in lateral thinking, in treating the mystery not like a real case but like a literary text, which, as readers know, it is: "Let's pretend everything to do with the Fieldings, even you and me sitting here now, is in a novel. A detective story. Yes? Somewhere there's someone writing us, we're not real" (221). She then comes up with several solutions and explanations as bookish possibilities. The most intriguing part of her discussion is that Fielding, dissatisfied with the character part he was saddled with, decided to take up authorship and write himself into a new story, which necessarily entailed writing himself out of the old one.

As the metafictional dimension of the story expands, readers are reminded of her literary connections. Isobel works for a publisher and has recently been involved with bringing out illustrated Victorian volumes. More significantly, she shares her surname with Lewis Carroll, the man who dropped Alice into Wonderland. And Fielding also carries the surname of a famous novelist; indeed, one of the themes of *Tom Jones* is the question of identity and finding out who one really is—it too is part detective story. Until she raises her literary possibilities, his name is mere happenstance, but once she makes Jennings explore the imaginative possibilities, the way humans must each be responsible for writing their own stories, then "Fielding" begins to take on added meaning. The story, in Isobel's hands, becomes the flip side of *Alice in Wonderland:* once the "main character," as she calls him, falls through the hole in the road, the ordinary world becomes a wonderland, a looking-glass world in which nothing is quite as it seems, in which one can no longer be certain about matters of identity and knowledge. When she suggests, for instance, that, "if our story disobeys the unreal literary rules, that might mean that it's truer to life" (223), Fowles uses her to develop the characters in his story and to critique the conventions that lead readers to expect, for instance, the tidy ending. He implies, through her analysis of Fielding, that characters do have a life of their own and that, like the lives of the readers, that life may be messy, untidy, without closure. She suggests, finally, that "nothing lasts like a mystery" (226), that Fielding has left his mark on the world by leaving it, which she compares to the absconding of the Supreme Author. From Fowles's existentialist position (which Isobel seems to share) the departure of God requires each of us to compose our own stories, our own lives.

The detective story, like any genre story, cannot stand much deconstructing before it begins to disintegrate. As Isobel weaves her fantastic explanations, the mystery (and Jennings's interest in solving it) evaporates, replaced by a love story between storyteller and audience. Jennings begins by seeing her as a sex object, noticing her breasts and wanting her in a way he hasn't wanted anyone recently. Yet, as she talks, she begins to come alive for him as a person, as an intellect and a spirit to reckon with. If he wants her sexually, she seduces him narratively. When at last, the mystery abandoned, they wind up in bed, the language refers humorously to his trade: she is "deprived" of her clothing "and proven, as suspected, quite defenseless underneath, though hardly a victim in what followed" (230–31). The narrative closes by suggesting that this surely unforeseen eventuality is the only concrete result of Fielding's disappearance, and yet it is quite enough. The relationship of Jennings and Isobel stands as the only genuinely human contact in the story, the only meeting in which the characters are really alive. Fielding has revealed a wasteland of intellect and feeling through his absconding, and Jennings has been appointed by New Scotland Yard to be the questing knight. It may be, as Carol Barnum has suggested, that the quest ultimately fails because Jennings and Isobel are too much of their own time, or that they "are not on the mythic journey,"[5] however much he may see her as a corn goddess. Yet the quester's true object is not the Grail but, rather, self-knowledge. In achieving a relationship beyond that seen among other characters, the two may have done what they can—all anyone can—to bring renewal to the wasteland.

If Jennings and Isobel represent the possibility of renewal, the characters in the succeeding story, "The Cloud," demonstrate the wasteland world without renewal. Fowlesian irony dominates the story, locating sterile and vapid people in a little Eden; he upends T. S. Eliot's version by placing his hollow characters in a lush and fertile setting, thereby heightening the discrepancies. Paul and Annabel Rogers; their young daughters, Candida and Emma; their television producer friend, Peter Hamilton, and his current starlet girlfriend, Sally; Peter's young son, Tom; and Bel's sister, Catherine, on holiday together in central France, have gone picnicking to a secluded spot near a river—another of Fowles's famous "green enclosures." Yet this is a spoiled paradise. It holds not one but two snakes, the first a grass snake the children find early in the story. Later Peter comes across a poisonous adder then sees Catherine, who enigmatically allows him to make love to her (who seduces whom, and why, is unclear). The conjunction of the serpent, knowledge (clearly sexual), and death—Catherine has probably followed her husband in committing suicide immediately after the meaningless sex with Peter—completes this tale of the Fall from the ideals of romance. Within this framework of tawdry behavior and genuine pain, Fowles sketches out several familiar themes: the inability to communicate, intertextuality, the presence of death as both a driving force and a possible outcome, the unknowability of the Other, and the failure of the quester vis-à-vis the damsel in distress.

The conversations are, for the most part, shallow and misleading, as characters hide or misrepresent their true selves, speaking of trivialities. They also speak in a sort of shorthand, so that, when they discuss what has happened to make Catherine so unhappy, the reader is left largely ignorant and is forced to surmise her history from their fragmentary rendering. Even the narrative possesses an incomplete quality, drawing heavily on the characters' thoughts without attributing them as such. This technique, Fowles's version of free indirect speech, bears considerable resemblance to Virginia Woolf's use of it in *Mrs. Dalloway,* especially in its use of the indeterminant *one:*

> One liked old Paul, for all his going on. One envied old Paul; very nicely, as what in essence one would like one day for oneself, did Bel. She was so unobvious. The dryness, the mock simplicity that took no one in; fifty Sallys in her little finger; and a smashing pair of tits, that dress last night. (277)

> It must be close. One thought of it even with Emma, since he is there, also waiting, every moment now. That is why one can't stand other people, they obscure him, they don't understand how

beautiful he is, now he has taken on the mask; so far from
skeleton. But smiling, alive, almost fleshed; just as intelligent,
beckoning. The other side. Peace, black peace. (278)

The first of these passages is from Peter—crass,
self-interested, sex obsessed. The second is from Catherine—
fraught with pain, also egocentric, unable to get beyond the Self,
death obsessed. These two passages occur shortly before they
encounter each other and suggest the mixed motives behind their
sex as well as the more general inability of the two to communicate: since neither can get outside the Self, neither is capable of
empathy or even of comprehension of the Other.

The two passages also reveal another of the narrative devices
that Fowles employs in the story, the mix of verb tenses. He has
already pointed out, in a footnote to *Eliduc,* Marie de France's
free hand with verb tenses as a normal device of the medieval
romance. And he has himself dabbled with mixed tenses at the
end of *The Magus* and in "The Ebony Tower." Yet he jumbles
them more sytematically in this story than in any previous effort.
In part such a strategy emphasizes Catherine's time confusion, in
which the present is less alluring than either the past, in which her
husband is still alive, or the deathly future from which he
beckons. The present-past mixture also points up Fowles's more
general sense of timelessness, which has been present throughout
his work. His metafictional interest makes him aware that a text
is always being written for the first time with each new reader,
even as it already exists for those who have previously encountered it. This story, then, anticipates the unstable verb tenses and
narrative viewpoints of his novel-in-process, *Daniel Martin.*

The story's time shifting underscores its use of intertextual strategies. The characters, members of the Fowlesian smart set, chart their lives with references from the Bible to *Hamlet* to *The Waste Land* to television programs. They understand Sally, for example, in terms of her standard acting role, the trendy, shallow girlfriend. When they spot the snake Peter remarks that it "proves it's paradise, I suppose." As Catherine watches some fishermen at the river, she recalls T. S. Eliot's "Hurry up please it's time. Goonight Bill. Goonight Lou. Goonight. Goonight" (247) from, significantly, *The Waste Land.* Like the speaker of Eliot's poem, she connects nothing with nothing. Her mind flits between the void of her life and the void of death. As she explains the theories of Roland Barthes to Peter, who is drawing her out for information for a possible television documentary, she explains that semiology studies the various sign systems by which humans communicate. Yet her tragedy is that she cannot communicate by any signs: the others are unwilling to hear her main story, about her husband's death, and they fail to grasp the signs she sends out. Only little Emma is willing to listen, and Catherine tells her a fairy tale.

That fairy tale reverses the intertextual strategies of the rest of the story, as Catherine charts her fiction with references to her own life as well as to fairy-tale conventions. Her story involves a princess who is lost and frightened of men. When she meets her prince she has no clothes nor a palace, so he cannot marry her. An old owl, who is a magician, permits her to have clothing or a palace, but not both, and, in trying to have one and then the other, she loses Prince Florio once again. They live in the forest in a kind of eternal present, in which they are both seventeen and in which she perpetually calls his name, the song of the oriole. Catherine tells Emma that she talked to the princess out in the woods before lunch. The story allows Catherine to dramatize her situation within a traditional narrative structure. She borrows elements from Ovid and the Brothers Grimm, yet the central features are her own: nakedness, homelessness, alienation, loss of the loved one, and the attempt at reunion with the lover. Emma notes that the story violates the genre by lacking a happy ending, but Catherine is incapable of providing one, since she sees no such possibility in the personal situation she is fictionalizing. Her final disappearance into mystery is couched in terms of the princess, the oriole, calling but no one being there now to hear her.

Throughout the story Catherine has been aware of her dead husband summoning her to join him, yet the final image arises from her story rather than from the larger fiction. While her fate goes unstated, the dark cloud—this story's manifestation of the ebony tower—suggests that she has joined her husband through suicide. Still, her fate remains forever suspended, in a now of indeterminacy, like the closing frieze of *The Magus.*

Like Isobel in the previous story, Catherine has the sense that she is in a novel, although she feels that the art form is no longer viable, that it sullies her. She is, then, both "writing and written" (279), both creating her situation and already created, contemplating the death readers do not see and having already achieved it. Like Sarah Woodruff, she exercises will in the midst of powerlessness, rejecting the text of her experience which society would write for her in favor of writing her own text, yet of course existing only in a text of Fowles's creation, in which her actions are not real but are, rather, metaphors for the real. That metaphorical level at which these stories operate may help

explain the sense of thinness of which some reviewers com-
plained when the book appeared or the general lack of attention
the book has received.[6] Still, the stories in *The Ebony Tower*
remain some of Fowles's most interesting and most thematically
revealing work.

Mantissa

Among all Fowles's fictions *Mantissa* stands alone in its
rejection of the mimetic level of narrative. Like some of the more
overt metafictions of Robert Coover or Italo Calvino, the tale
makes no efforts at realism. To be sure, all of Fowles's work has
contained a strong element of what Jerome Klinkowitz calls
self-apparency—reminders that this is, after all, an invented
thing and not a report of actual events.[7] Still, in his other work the
novelist has endeavored to tell stories contained by their texts. In
Mantissa the text is the story, or, rather, the story is of the text's
coming into being. As Pamela Cooper puts it, the text "chooses
vehemently to exclude external reality from the arena of narrative
action."[8] The action takes place entirely inside novelist Miles
Green's brain, and it concerns itself with bringing forth the text
of its own creation. Such circularity points to a strong element of
self-contemplation, even narcissism, with which Fowles charges
his writer-protagonist in this often hilarious tale of artistic production.
The ostensible action begins with an amnesia patient in
"Central" hospital—as such, it recalls Doris Lessing's *Briefing
for a Descent into Hell,* in which her main character is an amnesia
victim who awakes in London's Central Receiving Hospital—

UNDERSTANDING JOHN FOWLES

and the efforts of his female doctor to lead him back to memory. In fact, the patient here is Miles Green, novelist, and Dr. Delphie is in fact his muse, Erato. She has an assistant, a West Indian named Nurse Cory, later reputed to be the Dark Lady of Shakespeare's sonnets. Miles does not recognize his wife, Claire, nor have any memory of his name or his circumstances. The treatment the doctor and nurse undertake involves sexual awakening (no easy process, for Miles resists their efforts), which carries mnemonic awakening with it. Miles remembers more about himself, slowly, as he becomes more aroused, and he regains his power of speech as he is brought to erection. Readers may question the equation of sexual potency with linguistic ability, but the scene is handled with such comic timing and garish bad taste that they will be inclined—and it will not be the last time in the novel—not to take the equation seriously. When Miles is brought to climax by Dr. Delphie (he would have preferred Nurse Cory, revealing either a taste for exoticism—his analysis—or a racist impulse toward sexual power games), he brings forth, "gives birth to" in the text's terms, the text of the story that has just occurred. The chapter ends with the nurse beginning to read the story, whose opening is identical with the novel's, to the proud parent, but the reading is interrupted by a crash that signifies the change of direction for the next chapter.

Long before this point in the tale readers will discern that this is no ordinary novel. Certainly, at the chapter's ending they will reject any notion of the verisimilitude of the plot, and the rest of the novel bears out that rejection. Shapes shift, elements in the hospital room appear or disappear as the text demands, Erato's moods swing wildly from moment to moment. It turns out that this story is a game played by author and muse, that they play it repeatedly, and that they are working out thematic variations as well as arguing over their roles in the creative process. Erato's punk rock avenger disguise at the outset of the second chapter soon gives way to her traditional appearance complete with white tunic and saffron girdle. Later Erato tries her own hand at creativity, telling the story she would write if she were given free rein: Miles as dull businessman, Miles as homosexual, Erato as nun and saint. Since she is only playing out the role Miles permits her, however, she is not given free rein to write the story. Miles acts out his role as postmodern literary theorist, huffing about the role of the novelist and the unwritability of texts. Still later Erato claims to have been the Dark Lady of Shakespeare's sonnets and the writer of the *Odyssey.* In part 3 she reverts to her role of Dr. Delfie (a scrambling of *defile,* perhaps). In the final part Miles turns her into a Japanese geisha, perfectly submissive and sexually obliging. Each version of herself tries to evoke a response from Miles but is not in itself definitive.

More dangerous to readers is the temptation to take Miles himself or his exchanges with Erato as standing for Fowles's attitudes or views on his craft. Because he is a novelist, because he is, unlike Erato, a more or less conventionally drawn character, he may appear to be his creator's surrogate. Yet he is no more representative of Fowles than she is. In the third section of the book, for instance, Miles insists that there is no place for humor in serious contemporary fiction—this, in a novel that has at times been uproariously funny. Clearly, his view of humor does not square with Fowles's. Neither does his view of himself, of the importance and seriousness of the novelist. Fowles has characterized himself in two humorous guises in *The French Lieutenant's Woman,* and he has taken liberties with the novelist-as-God figure in *Daniel Martin,* in which the main character's inadequacy to write the novel that one is reading forms a major element of the fiction. Miles insists to Erato that writing about fiction has become much more important than writing fiction itself for the modern writer and that authors have nothing whatever to do with the writing of texts (118–19). Neither of these positions accurately reflects Fowles's own view of his vocation.

The problem, then, is how to construe the action of the novel, given that the novelist is a very different sort from Fowles himself and that the view of the creative process is substantially different. All of the shenanigans, sexual and otherwise, are designed to bring about endless versions of an ongoing story, a smutty tale of his own encounter with his muse. What he seeks to write is even more ethereal, an "unwritable," "unfinishable," "unimaginable," "endlessly revisable" "text without words."[9] Such self-reflexivity pushes beyond the metafictional impulses displayed in Fowles's real texts. Indeed, whatever reservations he may have about narrative closure, he has always delivered story in abundance, and those stories have always been about something larger than his own immediate experience as novelist. By comparison, Miles's work is thin and unengaging; he is a figure of satire, the novelist Fowles could have become with a bit less luck, perhaps. Miles gives his creator the opportunity to parody his own worst impulses and those of his contemporaries.

This parodic element makes the novel difficult to decode: When is Fowles being serious? What is his point? Does he have a point? Is the pornographic element an attribute of his character or himself? When Pamela Cooper attacks the book as pornographic, for instance, she does so by denying the distance between author and protagonist-author: "*Mantissa* acknowl-

edges that its author's view of artistic power is also a vision of
female sexuality which lends itself to both the pornographic
banalities of a Frederick Clegg and the more pretentiously
obscene imaginings of a Miles Green."[10] Such a reading of
Fowles can be undertaken, yet it requires a falsifying of both the
nature of his relation to his characters and to the element of comic
inversion in *Mantissa*. Neither Clegg nor Miles should be con-
strued as author surrogates, and, indeed, the view of female
sexuality which both employ (and here Clegg offers the clearer
example) stands as threatening to life or sanity. *The Collector*
represents an approach to sexuality and power which its creator
unqualifiedly rejects, as his depiction of the monstrous attitudes
of Clegg makes clear. The satirical rendering of Miles's sexual
attitudes is more subtle, yet it too is rejected. Fowles demonstrates the narcissistic, even masturbatory, character of Miles's
interactions with his muse and his range of subject matter to be
laughable.

Yet the exact nature of Fowles's involvement with this
novel remains problematic. His character shares certain experiences with him, such as a novel whose original twelve endings
were cut to three. The name Miles Green echoes the inverted
name Fowles, John. And, of course, the entire business of artists
and muses is familiar territory in the Fowlesian canon (it has been
explored most fully in "The Ebony Tower"). There is the problem, moreover, of just who is responsible for the text we are
reading: from the moment that Miles Green "gives birth" to his
story, which is the chapter we have just been reading, we can
never be sure whether Fowles has created the novel in his own
persona or in Miles's. Cooper, and she is not alone, would find
Fowles responsible for the whole. Mahmoud Salami asserts that

the two must be kept separate, largely on the strength of Miles's rejection of humor's place in current fiction.[11] Perhaps a more productive way to read the novel is as existing between invisible quotation marks. There is a gap between what is written and what is understood by what is written. As in any comic or satiric work written as if delivered by a character—here one might think of *Gulliver's Travels* or Flann O'Brien's comic work *At Swim-Two-Birds*—the text exists within an envelope of silence which acts as a commentary provided by the unspoken communication of author and reader. The ambiguous nature of the narrative in *Mantissa* is typical of Fowles's work. Readers will recognize the problem from interpreting Sarah in *The French Lieutenant's Woman* or resolving the final frieze of *The Magus*. Yet such ambiguity presents special problems when it touches so closely upon the character of the novelist himself and when the novelist has spent his career making himself unknowable.

What Fowles presents readers with in this, his most overtly postmodern work, is the difficulty caused by authorial play. Most critical strategies are predicated on textual earnestness or seriousness of purpose, and they assume seriousness, or at least straightforwardness, of tone as well. They assume, that is, the novel as literary *work*. There is a strain of contemporary literature, however, dedicated to play, to undercutting its own seriousness, to sending up the values it purports to espouse, to operating, as Salami puts it, through "games, fun, and comedy."[12] When last seen, for instance, Miles has just knocked himself out. He had been turned into a satyr and Erato into the wished-for geisha. As he leaps at her, she disappears, leaving him to crash headlong into the wall and to fall unconscious. Such a scene makes it difficult to speak definitively about Fowlesian attitudes regarding sexual relations, although one might conclude that his hero is a buffoon. So, too, with the padded walls that may be the gray matter of his own brain, although the padding looks rather like adolescent breasts: Ought one really to take such imagery seriously or join in the authorial mirth? The conclusion here might be that Miles is sex obsessed and that his search for creative inspiration is decidedly onanistic. In other words, when the writer satirizes the act of writing, the writing he presents becomes very slippery.

Nor is this accidental. Fowles has long resented the treatment he has received from academic critics and, indeed, the whole critical enterprise. We should not be surprised, then, if he offers up a text that is a mine field for the theoretical fraternity while a delight for the receptive reader. One of the acknowledged sources is Flann O'Brien. Part 4 opens with an epigraph adapted from *At Swim-Two-Birds,* and O'Brien receives direct mention and quotation in the closing pages. (O'Brien—one of whose other pen names was Myles—also took a dim view of academic criticism.) Like that book, *Mantissa* may at times feel insubstantial, not entirely serious, even silly. But it is an inspired silliness, a transporting lunacy, which drives the book and carries readers to the end.

Notes

1. John Fowles, *The Ebony Tower* (Boston: Little, Brown, 1974) 86. Subsequent references will be noted parenthetically.

2. Carol Barnum, *The Fiction of John Fowles: A Myth for Our Time* (Greenwood, Fla.: Penkeville, 1988) 85.

3. Fowles, *The Aristos* (Boston: Little, Brown, 1970) 192. Subsequent references will be noted parenthetically.

4. See, for instance, Robert Huffaker, *John Fowles* (Boston: Twayne, 1980) 125.

5. Barnum 94.

6. The collection is excluded, for instance, from discussion by both Katherine Tarbox, *The Art of John Fowles* (Athens: U of Georgia P, 1988); and the revised edition of Peter Wolfe, *John Fowles: Magus and Moralist* (Lewisburg, Pa.: Bucknell UP, 1979).

7. Jerome Klinkowitz. *The Self-Apparent Word: Fiction as Language / Language as Fiction* (Carbondale: Southern Illinois UP, 1984). Klinkowitz counterposes this term to *transparency,* the tendency of texts to hide their existence in order to stress the reality of the stories they carry.

8. Pamela Cooper, *The Fictions of John Fowles: Power, Creativity, Femininity* (Ottawa: U of Ottawa P, 1991) 205.

9. Fowles, *Mantissa* (Boston: Little, Brown, 1982) 161. Subsequent references will be noted parenthetically.

10. Cooper 210.

11. Mahmoud Salami, *John Fowles's Fiction and the Poetics of Postmodernism* (Rutherford, N.J.: Associated UP, 1992) 214.

12. Salami 214.

CHAPTER SIX

Daniel Martin: The Mature Fowlesian Novel

Middle age can manifest itself in a host of ways. It brings new concerns and new possibilities. For John Fowles *Daniel Martin* represents his engagement with those issues of middle age. The novel picks up themes, attitudes, and devices, reworking them through a mature perspective while at the same time exploring issues of aging, of confronting past mistakes, of deciding, as Robert Frost says, "what to make of a diminished thing." The exploration of Self (or potential selves) through choosing between opposed females, enchanted enclosures, the corrupting influence of modernity, the role of art and artists in society, the importance of the past to understanding the present—familiar themes all—make appearances in this book. Dan's relationships with Jenny and Jane recall the romantic dilemmas of both Charles Smithson and Nicholas Urfe, his discussions with the East German Egyptologist remind us of earlier, often cryptic conversations with mentor figures such as Maurice Conchis, Dr.

UNDERSTANDING JOHN FOWLES

Grogan, or Henry Breasley. Fowles toys with the reader through the author–character–character's alter ego identification games, blurring the distinctions between Fowles, Dan, and Dan's creation S. Wolfe (an anagram of Fowles). At the same time, *Daniel Martin* does not simply reiterate previous themes. Rather, it works through them from a decidedly middle-aged perspective, as both author and character have matured from the days of, say, *The Magus.* That maturity deepens and changes these issues from earlier works while at the same time investigating the same basic territory.

That the novel is the least well received of Fowles's full-length works can be attributed to its length, to its density, to its shifting narrative sands, and to its comparative lack of magic. His earlier works, while clearly postmodern, have about them an element of the miraculous, the fantastic, the fabulous, which allows readers to accept the gamesmanship of the narratives because the fiction has been removed from the arena of realism. *Daniel Martin,* on the other hand, demands that the reader hold both realism and metafiction in view at the same time; indeed, Robert Huffaker would classify the book not as realism but, instead, as naturalism.[1] For much of the novel he seems to have left his own world and entered that of Iris Murdoch—trendy upper-middle-class types involved in the media and the academy trotting around making messes of their lives, flirting with alternative belief systems and one another, looking for someone or something to love other than themselves. It even contains the requisite Murdochian philosopher, Dan's former brother-in-law Anthony, a terminal cancer patient who summons Dan back to England and promptly commits suicide, thereby setting the novel in motion. It comes as no surprise, therefore, when Jane confesses her two-year-long affair with one of Anthony's colleagues by calling it an "Iris Murdoch situation."[2] What the novel lacks, however, is Murdoch's sure authorial hand; her characters may lack control, but that failure is not shared by their creator.

Some readers of *Daniel Martin* may object to the mixing of conventional fictional materials, which suggests a certain narrative structure, with the highly unstable narrative structures that actually make up the novel. Like his other works, this book defies readerly expectations, in part because the expectations have to do with one of two stories being told. In a sense the real story is not the one about Dan and his love life, although that occupies the majority of narrative space. Rather, it has to do with Dan coming to grips with his past, his psyche, and his craft sufficiently to let him write this highly autobiographical novel. His rejection of screenwriting in favor of the novel sounds simple enough, but he must rid himself of the psychological and professional baggage of the Hollywood hack before he can begin. He has, after all, previously given up the relatively honest world of the stage for the corruption of the movies. Significantly, both activities exist in a kind of eternal present, and one of Dan's major struggles in the novel is to master verb tense and the understanding of the past which such mastery implies.

The novel begins, for instance, with a Hardyesque evocation of Dan's youth in Devon, yet the style is far from Hardy's. "The Harvest" details the events of the intersection of reaping wheat and of slaughtering rabbits trapped by the reaper's progressive inward sweep with the overflight by a German Heinkel bomber. The combination of terror and revulsion at the different forms of violence (one of the rabbits is sliced in half by the reaper but fails to die immediately, so he must dispatch it) sets Dan apart as a thinking and sensitive person. Even his superior diction marks him as different from his ungrammatical (and, by implication, unreflective) neighbors. Dan must escape into the beech woods to avoid the violence and to exercise his individual temperament, removing the gore from his knife blade by jamming it in the earth. In setting, dialogue, and action the scene owes much to Thomas Hardy, specifically to the rat-killing scene in *Tess of the D'Urbervilles*.[3] His mode of telling, however, is not that of the novel but, rather, of the screen: the present tense, the lack of perspective, the movement from the general group toward the single protagonist, camera and time directions such as the single-word paragraph "Later" (11), indeed even the tangential relation of the scene to the action that will follow—all of these elements suggest that we are reading the "hook" scene of a filmscript.

Throughout the novel Dan struggles with his materials, sometimes writing in the third person and the past tense, sometimes in first-person present, sometimes sliding between them, even incorporating, unreworked, the raw material of Jenny's letters. His apparent inability to control his fictional tools, even the basics of point of view and verb tense, suggests the difficulty that lies ahead of Dan in becoming a novelist. Jenny raises the prospect of his writing a novel in the second chapter, and it is mentioned frequently as one of Dan's goals throughout the book. The novel's final paragraph announces not his intention but, rather, his accomplishment: "That evening in Oxford, leaning beside Jane in her kitchen while she cooked supper for them, Dan

DANIEL MARTIN

told her with a suitable irony that at least he had found a last sentence for the novel he was never going to write. She laughed at such flagrant Irishry; which is perhaps why, in the end, and in the knowledge that Dan's novel can never be read, lies eternally in the future, his ill-concealed ghost has made that impossible last his own impossible first" (673). That last line propels the reader back to the beginning in a way that owes something in spirit, if not language, to Joyce's *Finnegans Wake:* "Whole sight, or all the rest is desolation" (1). The opening could well be the last line of his "impossible" novel; certainly, its placement as the first line is problematic—cryptic, detached, metaphorical in the midst of immediate detail, more of an epigraph than a proper opening line. The final paragraph also points out for any readers who somehow might have missed the fact that this is the novel that Dan cannot write, must learn to write. It is, then, what S. Kellman calls the "self-begetting" novel: that special, reflexive class of *Künstlerroman* in which the focus is the development of character to the point at which he or she can become not merely an artist but can write the novel one has just finished reading.[4] Fowles gives this type of novel a double twist. First, Dan's "novel" lacks the refinement that would make the work a finished product; that is, we are reading something more like the draft of the novel that he may yet be able to produce than the novel itself. And, second, there is the postmodernist concern with fictionality and intertextuality, as the novel plays off other texts, those both of Fowles and of other writers.[5]

Daniel Martin is an exceptionally well-read and well-traveled first novelist. His narrative invokes and plays off of a wide array of texts. In nearly all of Fowles's narratives, for instance, the sacred wood is invoked. In this tale Dan refers to the Robin Hood myth as the sanctioning prior text, along with Restif de la Bretonne's eighteenth-century autobiographical fiction, *Monsieur Nicolas.* The latter not only sanctions the use of autobiography in the novel, and vice versa, but also imports Fowles's own Monsieur Nicolas, Nicholas Urfe of *The Magus,* into the work. In the same vein Dan seeks to justify his career in film with the names of celebrated filmmakers: Ingmar Bergman, Luis Buñuel, Satyajit Ray. He cites them as instances of the kind of filmmaking which England has proved incapable of undertaking, yet their very mention is at another level an attempt to give his own considerably lesser efforts legitimacy. At the end of the same chapter in which all these artists are mentioned, "The Sacred Combe," Dan identifies the strain of modern fiction which most appeals to him as the one that runs from Henry James through Virginia Woolf and on through Vladimir Nabokov (294). Again, invoking the names of the greats may be an attempt at self-legitimatization; if so, it is fraught with great peril, for Dan will likely never be James or Woolf or Nabokov. Even for his creator the parallels hold a danger of being taken seriously, to his disfavor. When Hamlet gives his instructions to the players, Shakespeare knows the risks he runs of not living up to his own precepts. So, too, for any artist invoking his pantheon: he may come up short.

Elsewhere in the book Jane calls her affair an Iris Murdoch sort of thing; Anthony speaks disparagingly of Samuel Beckett; Byron is mentioned; Hardy is emulated; Antonio Gramsci is discussed; and Dan reads Georg Lukács on literary realism and romanticism, on Thomas Mann and Sir Walter Scott. These writers and their texts play upon and are played upon by the text

Dan is creating, with varying degrees of awareness on his part. Their effect is twofold: to reveal elements of Dan's artistic consciousness and to emphasize the fictionality of the enterprise. To be sure, *Daniel Martin* represents a greater involvement with realism than Fowles's earlier work. Yet one must never forget that it is also a work of metafiction, in which the interplay of narrative signs is highly self-conscious. References may point outward to "real-world" objects or situations, but they also point inward, toward the act of fictive creation, reminding readers that the work at hand is, after all, a product of the imagination and not a journalistic transcription of events in the world outside the text. The various literary references and parodies of the novel, then, form an internal sign system whose ultimate goal may be simply to remind us of their presence, as a means of insisting on the work's fictionality.

One other great author forms the central focus of the novel's intertextuality. As is his wont, Fowles consciously plays off his other works, particularly *The Magus,* in a number of situations and set pieces in the novel. Most important, of course, readers are confronted with an egoistic narrator. While Dan lacks Nicholas's self-certainty and smugness, he shares other significant traits. Both are cut off from their pasts; both have a long history of sexual relationships for which they deny responsibility (one of Dan's former lovers has committed suicide, whereas Alison's suicide is faked); both have dual affairs with similar women, one vulnerable and accessible, the other mysterious and resistant; both travel to exotic locales as they attempt to deal with malaise; both conclude or nearly conclude their stories with a meeting with the "accessible" lover in a London park; and both must learn to get beyond "I" in their thinking. Yet the novels are not coterminous. Dan's story differs in its insistence on middle-agedness: he must confront the failures of his lifetime as well as the successes. Unlike Nicholas, Dan has lived long enough to have had his character flaws make an impact on his world. His marriage to Nell failed, but it produced a daughter, Caroline, as well as acrimony and estrangement from Nell's sister, Jane, and her husband, Anthony. His career as a playwright went from early success to dissatisfaction and rejection (including rejection by family and friends over his drama *à clef* based on his marital breakup) to a shift to Hollywood. That move suggests a refusal to assume responsibility for his work, as his other behavior suggests a similar refusal for responsibility for his personal situation. Whereas Nicholas attempts to cast his difficulties in specifically existentialist terms, however, Dan's past is too cluttered to permit the man-alone stance.

There is, similarly, a disjunction between the issues that drive the novels. *The Magus* revolves around the existential and moral crises—can this man be saved? can he learn to be a responsible adult? *Daniel Martin,* on the other hand, explores those characterological issues within the context of saving (or developing) vision, as the novel's opening sentence suggests— can this man acquire sight sufficient to the task of becoming an artist?—vision to accompany his talents, to sustain him through the arduous process of novelistic becoming. It may be that these two sets of issues are both subsets of the ethical realm and are therefore more closely related than they at first appear. To be sure, Fowles has mingled narrative development and personal development throughout his work. The two works, then, become flip sides of the same coin: Nicholas, in telling his story, is composing his life; Dan, in recounting his life, is composing his novel. Still, it is important to recognize the different aims and purposes of the two books as well as their similarities.

The novel's first four chapters lay out the novel's working plan: Dan's personal situation, the technical and mnemonic difficulties confronting him, and the varied narrative timescapes.[6] The first chapter, "Harvest," recounts that long-ago day when farmwork and slaughter combined to push the sensitive young Dan to seek escape in his own secret combe, the beechwood above the fields. The second chapter brings the story into the present, in which his lover, Jenny, proposes that he write a novel. Her view is that the process is comparatively simple: since he has enough money not to worry, he can easily make time, which is the other necessity. She even picks out his pen name, Simon Wolfe, from the phone directory. Dan, meanwhile, is resistant, hesitant, self-denying, dismissive, in a scene still being written in the grammar of film, with mentions of film star girlfriends and "beat" pauses, and still in the third-person present tense of film scripts. Jenny predicts something will happen, "a door in the wall" will open, providing him with the impetus to write his novel. At the end of the chapter Dan receives a phone call that turns out to be, in the still-too-neat world of film logic, the opening door.

Readers are kept in suspense, however, until the beginning of chapter 5, as Fowles lays out Dan's world in two intervening chapters. The first of those, "The Woman in the Reeds," recalls a day at Oxford in 1950 which Dan and Jane spent punting on the river, when they found, instead of a quiet place to study, a woman's decomposing body. In a reprise of the earlier chapter an American bomber flies low overhead, again merging the local death with its more universal counterpart. Like the earlier harvest scene, this flashback exists chiefly to establish milieu and sensibility, but this one also begins to give Dan and Jane a history of their own, independent of future spouses Nell and Anthony: a shared secret, a clear mutual attraction, a profound experience. This closeness will develop further in Dan's rooms three chapters later, culminating three chapters after that with largely unsatisfactory lovemaking, which Dan interprets as an act of exorcism on Jane's part. The distance between these related scenes suggests the difficulties Dan encounters in marshaling his narrative forces.

The fourth chapter presents clear evidence of his narrative difficulties. In it, "An Unbiased View," Jenny presents the first of her interpolations, in this case her version of their first meeting, of the personnel involved in the current film project, of their first date and lovemaking. Yet she calls it pure fiction. Later she will write of an erotic experience with her costar then retract that as fiction. Throughout her additions to the text the issues of veracity and fictionality make interpretation difficult: Is she telling the truth or not, or, rather, what sort of truth is she telling? What it presents in film terms is the change in perspective (one can almost see the script direction NEW POV), the attempt to emulate objectivity by overcoming the camera's inevitably limiting, subjective focus. This chapter does not so much lead into as give way to the conclusion of Dan's phone call, in "The Door." Returning again to third-person present, the narrative reveals the chief plot device: the dying Anthony, now beyond all hope, has asked to see Dan once more, to clear up "unfinished business." That requested visit pushes him back into his past, making him confront both the life he has fled in coming to Hollywood and his need to give it shape and resonance, his need to write his novel because the pat structures of film can never contain a life.

DANIEL MARTIN

These first five chapters form a sort of prologue to the action of the novel to follow, in the way the first act operates in a Hollywood movie. We are given the "hook" scene in "Harvest," followed by a scene to establish the main concern (Dan's attempt to write a novel), a flashback to "that day" in Oxford, a point-of-view shift to Jenny, and the phone call that spins the action off toward the main plot. This last chapter acts as the "plot point" in Hollywood parlance, pointing the way toward the central concerns and conflicts; this will not be the story of Dan and Jenny after all, it says. They may still believe it will be, but they are mistaken, as Jenny is when she tells Dan, in the second chapter, that their discussion will be chapter 1 of his novel. And, indeed, it would be the opening of the novel in which Jenny believes herself to be placed. She simply happens to be in a different novel.

This plot point also functions as a technique point: in the chapters that follow the narrative becomes radically unstable. Through these first chapters, perhaps because they deal in some way with Dan's movie-land identity, the viewpoint and verb tense remain comparatively constant. With the exception of Jenny's "contribution," the narrative technique of the screenplay predominates. From this point on, however, the viewpoint and verb tenses become quite slippery, changing from chapter to chapter and frequently within chapters. Nor are they predictable. Dan sometimes seems to slide into third person in moments of great personal tension, yet "Beyond the Door," in which they receive word of Anthony's suicide, maintains a first-person viewpoint throughout the period of shock then reverts to the third person when Dan is alone.

In returning to England, Dan must engage the consequences of his life. Indeed, he must return to a world in which
actions have consequences; his Hollywood life resembles a
fantasy existence, in which jobs are temporary, the products
ephemeral, love affairs momentary and terminated without recriminations, even living arrangements impermanent. England,
by contrast, represents both responsibility and rootedness. He
first confronts the California-England dichotomy of his life
through an encounter with Barney Dillon, an old classmate
whose life travesties Dan's. Barney works as a presenter on
television, the only medium Dan can think of as less substantial
than his own. Worse, while still married, he is having an affair
with his secretary, Dan's daughter, Caroline. That Caro, as she is
known, is almost the same age as Jenny McNeil (and still thought
of by her father as a confused adolescent) is an irony not lost on
Dan. The remainder of his trip, until Anthony's suicide at least,
constitutes a confronting of the past: suspicion on all sides,
too-overt attempts at politeness, denial that old injuries still give
pain, awkward conversation, guilt.

His first conversation with Jane is a small masterpiece of
obfuscation and public school shorthand meant to be long on
decency and utterly lacking in frankness. Sentences end before
the statements they seem to contain; answers to questions are
evasions masked as simple declarative sentences. The Chekhovian
quality of the dialogue may be indicative of Dan's background as
a playwright, but also, especially when compared with the
openness of his New World conversations with Jenny, it may
point to the bankruptcy of a certain kind of Englishness, the
clubby Oxbridge milieu in which honesty and forthrightness may
be considered bad form. Virtually everyone Dan speaks to during

this period shares his own experience—his ex-wife, Nell, and her new husband, Andrew, Jane, Anthony, Barney Dillon. Their conversations are routinely evasive, noncommittal, cryptic. His dealings with other classes—his rural caretakers, Ben and Phoebe; his first love, Nancy Reed; and the cockney twins, Miriam and Marjory, who become his lovers—typically involve greater frankness and psychological intimacy. The novel, like *The Collector* before it, seems to be asking a slightly different question from Forster's *Howards End:* not "Who shall inherit England" but "What sort of England is worth inheriting?" Ultimately, Dan and Jane cannot achieve any sort of real relationship until they leave England. In Egypt they find themselves freed from the common social constraints sufficiently to move toward honesty, although even that is a slow process. Still, without physically escaping Oxford and Compton (Andrew's estate), which stand for that oppressive form of Englishness, no personal progress would be possible.

Why Anthony summons Dan to Oxford remains rather fuzzy; certainly, he has wished to make peace, yet he also seems to have designs on Dan's future. Anthony attempts to clear up old misunderstandings and wounds, but his methods are unclear to Dan. He claims, for instance, that Dan wrongly assumed that Anthony was the wounded party in Dan and Jane's Oxford dalliance, implying without stating that Dan was badly used as well. Jane's insistence on confessing their sin (without consulting Dan) to Anthony did indeed place Dan in an awkward situation. Similarly, Dan's drama *à clef* is pronounced ancient history and the resulting rift only partly his fault. Strange, then, that Anthony should see Dan as Jane's "Good Samaritan," as he says, that he should believe his long-estranged brother-in-law as the one person capable of offering solace. At the same time, Anthony seems determined to condemn himself for his failures, especially for his inability to achieve "whole sight." He says he believes he may bequeath one "last mystical catch-phrase to the world" (194), and the reader recalls the opening line of the novel, realizing that he has done so. In terms of the master structure of the Fowlesian novel, Anthony's request acts as the summons or invitation that sends the protagonist's life—and the plot—off in a new direction. Like Nicholas Urfe's arrival at Bourani in *The Magus* or Charles's mandated attendance at Mrs. Poulteney's tea, this deathbed summons lifts the protagonist out of the aimlessness of his day-to-day life and forces him to focus on larger issues.

Anthony's death, then, separates the first and second parts of the novel, with the second leading up to the trip to Egypt, that journey forming the third part of the novel. Each section occupies approximately one third of the whole text. What follows the suicide is not so much consequence as revaluation. Dan must work his way through his own history, through his relationships and disappointments and through his difficulty in getting Jane to agree to accompany him on his trip. That working-through stands as a catalog of his memories of loss and folly, couched chiefly in paired figures and experiences. In the manner of the autobiographical novel there is the de rigueur recollection of his first tentative explorations of love and sexuality with Nancy Reed, the daughter of the wealthy farmer for whom he sometimes worked as a youth on the farm, Thorncombe, which he subsequently buys. Her sudden removal from his life (when the families get wind of the romance) echoes the loss in very early childhood of his mother, and the two, Dan's narrative suggests, go a long way to explain his difficulty in establishing permanent relationships with women. His experience with Nancy, he later says, formed the pattern for his subsequent involvement with women (615).

That pairing is only one of many in his story of himself. His affair with Andrea parallels his marriage in its domesticity, while his eight-week fling with the twins provides a shadow to his affair with Jenny, both in terms of her youth and of the impermanence of the arrangement. Caro's affair with Barney Dillon clearly parallels Dan's with Jenny; while he tries to pretend there is a difference in that Barney is still married, even that reminds him that he, too, was an unfaithful husband. Caro even has her own double, Jane and Anthony's daughter, Rosamund, a sort of ideal daughter who carries less emotional baggage and with whom Dan can have less guarded conversations. Even the landscapes are paired. Tsankawi, the Native American ruin in New Mexico, finds its complement in the Syrian ghost town of Palmyra: while Jenny and Dan find their sacred place in the first, Jane and Dan arrive at an entente culminating in sex in the second. Dan has attempted to recreate the sacred wood, the green enclosure of his memory, by buying Thorncombe, yet that act is arbitrary, willful, and ultimately unsuccessful. One cannot will oneself back to innocence. Instead, he finds that sacred place on Kitchener's island, a "green place out of time, a womb, where all had seemed potential" (613). The narrative moves forward by these pairings and oppositions, which operate by creating emphases and tensions that articulate the novel's concerns and intentions.

Curiously, the novel's narrative disarray begins to sort itself out when Dan embarks on the trip that is ostensibly film driven: his journey to Egypt is undertaken to finish his screenplay on Lord Kitchener and to scout out shooting locations. This oddity is only one of many ironies in the book's final third. The script's subject, Horatio Herbert Kitchener, earl of Khartoum, conquerer of the Sudan, secretary of war at the outset of World War I, represents a version of Englishness—the British version: militarist, imperialist, colonialist—which Fowles clearly rejects. At the same time, however, that colonialist past affords Dan the opportunity to make this particular trip into antiquity, and in that sense its existence is providential, just as the highly suspect film industry (which has not always been kind to Fowles's work) provides Dan with the livelihood and the mobility to undertake such a journey. His story, of course, like his "novel," is only tangentially related to the activity that occasions it.

Once the journey through the Levant begins the narrative stabilizes into the conventional literary third-person, past-tense viewpoint, as if, whatever Dan's uncertainties on the personal or professional front, those of his storytelling manner have evaporated. Indeed, this may be a commentary on the streamlining of his life as well as his novelistic program: in going to Egypt with Jane, he leaves behind many of his personal difficulties—Jenny, Caro, former lovers, rivals, business concerns. The narrative establishes the relationship of Dan and Jane as its chief interest, stripping away by means of geography other distractions and concerns. While this does not simplify the nature of their relationship, it does focus the story's attention firmly on that single arena.

That attention also leads to a consideration of mature love and to the central character's main problem. It may be said without too much exaggeration that all of Fowles's male protagonists are variations on Nicholas Urfe, the hero of *The Magus;* certainly, they are all wrestling with the same set of issues and concerns. Daniel Martin, however, stands alone as the sole instance of that figure in middle age. The sorts of resolutions that have been plausible for Nicholas or Charles Smithson or David Williams will not suffice for Dan. Each of those earlier men winds up in a romantic frieze at or very near the end of his story; from there the question boils down to a fairly simple yes or no— will she accept him or not? will he have the strength of character to change or not? which outcome does the reader prefer? In the tradition of the bildungsroman (the novel of growth and development) the protagonist must grow to the point at which he is worthy of adult status, typically portrayed (in Fowles's work, in any case) as the point at which he can identify the "right" woman and also at which she will accept him. Dan, while going through this process of becoming, must seek more than acceptance. For the other protagonists the sexual Other is so alien, so incomprehensible, that mere acceptance is the most that can be hoped for. Fowles implies, on the other hand, that the mature hero should be expected to get farther than the first stage of a mating ritual. Dan must grow toward understanding. The bafflement of Nicholas, Charles, or David at the close of their fictions will not do in this case.

Jane is just as complex as her earlier (and younger) counterparts, by turns coy and frank, demure and demanding, solitary and gregarious, reserved and forward, hostile and loving. Yet her behavior is governed in part by Dan's presence, for, as he well knows, their relationship carries a great deal of baggage: the sexual attraction at Oxford, Dan's failed marriage to her sister, the autobiographical play and its fallout, the deathbed summons and reconciliation. While he may find her actions puzzling, he recognizes that there is often a reason lying behind the mystery.

Moreover, in order to choose between the open and accommodating Jenny and the moody Jane, he must arrive at a deeper understanding of all the parties involved than that required of, say, Charles Smithson. Clearly, the choice between Ernestina and Sarah is no choice, the former being so obviously marked for jilting. The movement of the entire last third of the novel is toward isolation of Dan and Jane with a view toward allowing him to begin to understand her more fully. They move through the same dance of mystification and revelation as Fowles's earlier heroes and heroines but with fewer devices to fall back on. The shift from London to Cairo to Aswan to Palmyra brings with it a progressive limiting of options: the masks of civility and convention fail in such unconventional settings. Dan and Jane have experienced events and places fraught with archetypal significance: the Nile itself, the safe green enclosure of Kitchener's island, the temple complex of Kom Ombo, their encounter with the mentor figure of Professor Kirnberger (who shares with Dan an interest in bird watching), a bedraggled bitch and her pups among the ruins at Palmyra. To these last Jane has a profound reaction, moved to tears and solicitous feeling, although she does not understand the mother's apparent abandonment (which Dan identifies as distraction behavior, trying to lure the perceived attackers, Dan and Jane, away from the pups). Dan thinks of them that "the gods take strange shapes; find strange times and stranger climates for their truths" (651). These archetypal experiences grind away at the modern selves until the inner, affective selves are quite near the surface. They achieve a state that in *The Magus* requires great artifice to produce; all of Conchis's devices and plots strive to bring Nicholas to such intimate contact with his inner being, with his moral center. Dan finds his on the trip, with a little help from the Marxist critic Georg Lukács's *Studies in European Realism.* Yet what he appreciates in Lukács is not the ideological sense that has informed Jane's thinking in recent years but, rather, the appeal to whole sight (taking us back to the opening sentence). Lukács valorizes Thomas Mann over Franz Kafka, for instance, because Mann's realism offers a more complete picture of the human condition than (as he sees it) the fragmentary, incomplete naturalism of Kafka and the modernists. Dan's struggle toward becoming a novelist has been a struggle to understand human beings in their wholeness; as a beginning, he must understand Jane in her wholeness. If Jane's acceptance of him is tentative and provisional, he must learn to live within its limits. He finds that the emotional life between people is untidy but that untidiness is not terminal, as he seems to have believed before, when he has wanted simplicity in relationships. Jane is teaching him complexity, and perhaps an appreciation of complexity.

When he returns to Jenny very near the end of the novel, the standard will-they-or-won't-they question of the earlier novels has vanished. Dan and Jenny are through. While they go through many of the same motions as the other couples (Hampstead Heath substituted for Nicholas's Regents Park), complete with the frozen moment, the issue of parting has already been resolved. Both of them know full well that they are saying good-bye. The novel closes, then, not with a romantic cliff-hanger but, instead, with an ordinary domestic scene in Jane's kitchen in Oxford. Dan and Jane may have a relationship that is contingent and uncertain, yet it takes on a kind of settled quality from its setting. And the talk is of the future, of the last line of the novel Dan claims he will never write.

UNDERSTANDING JOHN FOWLES

His claim, and the closing sentence's assertion that "that impossible last [has become] his own impossible first" (673), brings readers full circle, reminding them that this is Dan's novel, after all. The narrative regularity of the final third of the book may have lulled readers into ignoring the artistic problems and concerns Dan has had throughout, although Lukács's presence has kept the issue alive, but ultimately the artist's crisis remains. What Fowles reveals through this ending is that there only appear to be two subplots, the romantic and the artistic. In the final analysis they are one: in order to write his novel Dan must learn how to live; in order to write about fictional people he must begin to understand their living and breathing counterparts. Fowles, who holds scant respect for Marxism, has intuited the greatness in Lukács, that his thought so far transcends his system. *Daniel Martin,* by far Fowles's most realistic work, follows its opening sentence in embracing whole sight, in insisting that the writer must be a complete person, must overcome falseness and shallowness if he hopes to become an artist.

Notes

1. Robert Huffaker, *John Fowles* (Boston: Twayne, 1980).

2. John Fowles, *Daniel Martin* (Boston: Little, Brown, 1977) 218. Subsequent references will be noted parenthetically.

3. James R. Aubrey, *John Fowles: A Reference Companion* (New York: Greenwood, 1991) 118.

4. S. Kellman, "The Fiction of Self-Begetting," *Modern Language Notes* 91 (Dec. 1976).

DANIEL MARTIN

5. For a fuller discussion of the novel's postmodernist tendencies, including its intertextuality, see Mahmoud Salami, *John Fowles's Fiction and the Poetics of Postmodernism* (Rutherford, N.J.: Fairleigh Dickinson UP, 1992) 159–90.

6. See H. W. Fawkner, *The Timescapes of John Fowles* (Rutherford, N.J.: Fairleigh Dickinson UP, 1984) 61–66, for a discussion of the various pasts in the novel and the uses to which they are put.

CHAPTER SEVEN

A Maggot: Narrative Invention and Conventional Storytelling

Each of Fowles's books is filled with literary allusions, puns, teasers, sly references, and borrowings that place the story in a literary historical context. Yet that context is sometimes established only to be undermined and subverted. For instance, if *The Magus* reflects *The Tempest,* as the narrative and indeed the characters insist, it does so in a funhouse mirror. Similarly, *A Maggot* plays with the conventions of the novel of detection (already given Fowlesian treatment in "The Enigma") overlapping with a science fiction thriller, yet the result is neither Dashiell Hammett or H. G. Wells. The investigations of Henry Ayscough, limited as they are by his rationalist mind-set, form the center of the novel and lead to his encounters with the prostitute, Fanny/Louise/Rebecca, and her story, which cannot be rationally apprehended or empirically verified. The novel is a play of forms: interrogative transcripts, letters, depositions, newspaper facsimiles, all interspersed with conventional narrative. In other words, on one level the novel is a quite typical postmodernist stew. At the same time it is a profoundly human story of life, death, and spiritual transformation.

What is the relation of the narrative to the philosophy? That is, how do the narrative strategies of the novel reflect an emphasis on subjectivity? How do they draw out readers' subjective responses to the characters? The book makes strong demands for active reading, for the audience to react either positively or negatively to a host of situations. How readers interpret the ambiguous, in this case unknowable, ending of the novel, as suggested in earlier chapters, reflects not only textual cues but also psychological and philosophical elements of the readers themselves.

Fowles engages in many of the metafictional and self-deconstructive narrative devices of his contemporaries yet in a much more traditionally coherent structure than that of, say, Robert Coover or Italo Calvino. Throughout the novel, for instance, characters mention feeling as if they are but characters in a play or novel, and indeed the disappeared young nobleman has concocted a play of sorts, in which he and his hirelings play roles in what Maurice Conchis in *The Magus* calls a "theatre without proscenium." Further, the novel is made up of overlapping, often competing narratives: sworn depositions, letters, authorial narrative, false leads, corrections and emendations. Yet the structure of the book is such that the swirling array of narratives calls little attention to itself as postmodern gamesmanship. Rather, it reminds readers of the origins of the novel. In the eighteenth century, with few antecedents, the novel was experimental. Attempting to find its way in the absence of formula, it raided forms from a host of nonfictional sources—letters, histories, confessions, travelogues, diaries—and often presented those forms as being apparently unreworked raw materials. Our modern notions of the "conventional," or "traditional," novel derive chiefly from the nineteenth century, when economic forces in publishing created a highly regular, linear form. Those forces, however, did not make themselves felt until the 1840s, fully one hundred years after the setting of *A Maggot*. In the profusion of his forms, then, Fowles has harkened back to the roots of the English novel.

The novel begins with a lengthy narrative concerning a group of travelers through southwestern England in 1736. Indeed, it opens with a frieze of the travelers, the image Fowles claims in the prologue to have haunted him for several years prior to writing the book. The novel itself parallels the course of its writing: a story is suggested, then adumbrated, then fleshed out by degrees until eventually an ending, however tenuous, is reached. The opening narrative runs some fifty pages, yet it covers only the last known day of the group's sojourn. On this day, and this evening, comparatively little happens of external note, yet much is fraught with significance.

The travelers are five: a Mr. Bartholomew, his uncle, his deaf-mute manservant, a guard named Sgt. Farthing, and a maidservant named Louise. They are first seen on a dismal final day of April. The opening rings with phrases that could come straight out of Poe, especially "The Fall of the House of Usher": "the bleak landscape," "an aura of dismal monotony," "a waste of dead heather and ling."[1] These phrases, lifted from the Gothic imagination, provide a sense of foreboding and of immanent dark occurrences. When the novel reveals a tale of death and disappearance, readers' suspicions are confirmed: this is a Gothic novel full of event and magic and evil.

The last day the five spend together, however, is largely without event. They travel to a town identified, in the manner of the period's own novels, only as C———, put up for the night in Thomas Puddicombe's inn, and stay till morning. There Farthing boasts and struts below-stairs in the kitchen, evidently hoping for a sexual conquest of one of the maids. Above, the local vicar comes to call, received by the uncle, although not by Mr. Bartholomew. Dick Thurlow, the deaf-mute, performs his master's bidding, although he makes sexual advances toward the maidservant. Louise herself, meanwhile, changes attire completely and attends to Mr. Bartholomew's chamber, where she is revealed to be a London prostitute named Fanny. We learn that Mr. Bartholomew has bought her services for three weeks, and, although he has not availed himself of her sexual favors, he has given her to Dick. Indeed, Bartholomew seems most ambivalent toward Fanny, ranting about her eternal damnation for her sins, seeming horrified of fleshly pleasure, while also capable of momentary great tenderness toward her. He speaks of great events on the morrow, although he is quite mysterious about what sort of events. In his talks with his uncle, Bartholomew has revealed that the others present are servants hired for show to escort him to some shadowy end point. The uncle himself is really an actor named Francis Lacy, who has been given his role and has hired Farthing yet who knows nothing of Fanny/Louise's part or of Bartholomew's ultimate subterfuge. Lacy is distressed at his lack of knowledge and the dangerous nature of his employer's hints. Bartholomew will say only that he is seeking cosmic mysteries, suggesting that he may see into the future. Beyond that, however, he hides behind a tissue of metaphors and evasions, speaking of meeting his muse, of a play without an ending. He is remarkably unforthcoming, although he seems at times to wish to unburden himself. He does tell Lacy that his part will be discharged the next day, once they have escaped the town without being discovered. The narrative section ends with a great sense of expectation, although for what the text does not say.

The next document to come to light is a newspaper article of nearly two months later, stating that Dick has been found hanged with his mouth stuffed with violets and that the rest of the party has disappeared and is presumed murdered, probably by Dick himself.

These, then, are the last known facts. From this point on the novel relies on conjecture, hearsay, testimony from witnesses who may or may not be trusted and who may or may not have received their information firsthand or with clear vision. The progression of witnesses under examination is obviously artificial, progressing from least knowledgeable to most, from the innkeeper Puddicombe and his maid to, finally, Fanny herself, born Rebecca Hocknell, now married and, in her ultimate renaming, known as Rebecca Lee. In life, of course, an investigation rarely proceeds from tangent to center in such an orderly fashion, with each piece of testimony pushing inward another step toward the truth. This strategy is one of several ways in which Fowles reminds readers that the novel is all artifice—that, however compelling the story may be, its strength is as *story*.

As in *The French Lieutenant's Woman,* he employs various devices that call attention to the modernity of the narrative, as against the historicity of the events of the narrative. The devices are more subtle in *A Maggot,* but they are present. He again uses the modern corollary to focus readers' attention on the action and, simultaneously, to distance them from it. At several points the narrative compares Henry Ayscough to his modern counterparts, invariably showing the radical changes between the ages. Similar comparisons are made between Rebecca or John Lee or James Wardley and people of our time or of the future. When Fowles says of Wardley, for instance, that in him "the spirit of Tom Paine . . . is alive" (393), readers must recognize a spirit of great prescience, since Paine was not born until the next year, 1737. The novelist continues his fondness for taking history into the future, as when, in the midst of Farthing's boasting, he points out that the Admiral Byng to whom Farthing refers is not the Admiral Byng who died ingloriously in 1757 but, rather, the father of that one (29–30). Fowles also revels in comparisons of the attitudes of the two centuries. He notes that the eighteenth century hated wildness in nature or elsewhere (9–10), implying, as he does in *The French Lieutenant's Woman,* that twentieth-century English people have changed attitudes entirely. Most important, attitudes toward the Self have altered dramatically over two and a half centuries. Fowles emphasizes at several points that the characters, regardless of class, lack a highly developed sense of Self. They may have an innate belief in their superiority, as does Ayscough, but that comes from membership in his class rather than from any feelings of his own self-worth. The major informing philosophy behind Fowles's work, existentialism, would be completely alien and incomprehensible to the characters in the novel. Indeed, the early glimmer of a sense of Self becomes an important issue in the novel.

Two further reminders of the modernity of the narrative remain. The first is the technological understanding required to appreciate Rebecca's "vision," or "experience." She describes to Ayscough a number of devices that are quite beyond the ability of either of them to comprehend: telescreens, military tanks and bombers, electronic control panels, spaceships. None of this, however, is particularly remarkable to contemporary readers. While the net effect may be mysterious or even beyond belief, none of the individual marvels exceeds our conceptual ability. And, finally, the prologue and epilogue, with their emphasis on the writer and his motives, tend to distance readers from the narrative. In the very brief prologue he explains the original conception of the novel as a single image of cloaked riders who never seem to go anywhere. The purpose of the novel becomes clear at that point: the writer has had to cause the riders to arrive somewhere and to explain their journey. The epilogue teases out an outcome for the novel beyond the story proper and brings its philosophical weight to bear: the novel is not so much a working out of existentialism as it is an exploration of the first glimmerings of individuality and private responsibility in Western consciousness which make existentialism possible. The surprising revelation in the epilogue—that this story has involved the mother of Mother Ann Lee, founder of the Shakers, and that this tale has been written by an atheist—tends to push the reader away from naive acceptance of the story as story.

That surprise, however, is merely the last of many small jolts to readerly sensibilities, of shifts in approach. The major shift occurs early on, when the external narrative breaks off, replaced by a series of depositions taken by Henry Ayscough.

A MAGGOT

The comforting certainties of third-person narrative evaporate, replaced by the jouncier rhythms of question-and-answer "primary" documents, with their necessarily attendant problems of subjectivity and narrative fallibility. In a sense the remainder of the novel brings together Fowles's career-long obsession with point of view as a determinant of narrative reality. The struggle between Ferdinand and Miranda in *The Collector,* for instance, has as much to do with gaining narrative supremacy as it does with their physical and psychological warfare: the matter centers on whose reality, whose subjective version, will triumph. In *The Magus* Nicholas Urfe's failure as an artist, and as a human being, stems from his inability to envision any viewpoint but his own, to escape his obsessive subjectivity far enough to embrace compassion or empathy. In *A Maggot* subjective accounts of the events of the story are placed against Ayscough's equally subjective doubts and criticisms about those accounts and their bearers. In "The Man on the Dump," when Wallace Stevens asks, "Where was it one first heard of the truth?" the answer is "The the."[2] The progression of narratives in the novel reinforces this modern bias against that definite article; truth becomes essentially unknowable in the absence of empirically verifiable data.

The first two witnesses interrogated by Ayscough know very little of the story. Thomas Puddicombe, landlord of the Black Hart Inn (the name itself adding to the pseudo-Gothic elements of the early novel), and his maid, Dorcas Heller, are able to attest chiefly to the efficacy of the Bartholomew ruse. They are, indeed, the intended audience for the young lord's play without walls—people met along the journey who will uncritically accept the identities of the passersby. It is specifically for Puddicombe and Dorcas that David Jones, as Farthing, plays his part as miles gloriosus, or military boaster, complete with tales of naval heroics and a sexual advance toward the maid. They meet the elder gentleman in his guise as uncle and watch him receive the local clergyman, certainly evidence of his social standing. Puddicombe is able to supply one or two salient details, chiefly that Farthing, recognized as a hollow braggart, slips off in the early hours of the morning, not to return. He is, therefore, not with the party when it departs. This intelligence, however, does not reduce the mystery; it increases it. Why would the armed escort desert the travelers on the very morning of their disappearance? Does he have prior knowledge of their fate? Does he cause it? These questions occur to Ayscough, requiring him to find Farthing.

Dorcas Heller provides further curious details. Bartholomew has traveled with considerable baggage, most notably a small wooden, brassbound chest that was the subject of much speculation among the inn's staff. Some believe it contains gold, but Dorcas discovers that it contains strange papers, as she tells Ayscough: "Us saw one, 'twas a great circle, and another with three sides, and marks like the moon. . . . Like a cheese-rind, sir, or the black in the old moon" (77). There is also a large brass instrument like a clock, full of wheels and gears, although the face of it remains hidden. Dorcas, however, is too ignorant and inarticulate to be able to know or explain what she has seen. Bartholomew's papers are covered with arcana, of presumably zodiacal or alchemical origins, although clearly turned to his own uses. Her other useful piece of information consists of having noticed Louise late at night talking in Bartholomew's room and then creeping back into her own room much later. Remarkably, to Ayscough, the nature of the meeting is not sexual, for, Dorcas reports, the bed is not slept in that night—lain on, yes, but never turned back.

Ayscough's astonishment underscores a basic theme of his interrogations: that the nature of his lordship's escapade must be sexual and perverse. This conclusion follows logically from the known facts. Great secrecy surrounds the journey: his lordship insists on false identities for all concerned; he has hired both a known prostitute and an actor—and this at a time when the Puritan belief that the theater was a center for licentiousness, a belief that had led to the closing of the theaters a century before, still lingered—actors being little better than prostitutes themselves; the prostitute is known to have frequented his room unescorted; the party disappears into the wilds of Devon. Ayscough, a product of the rationalism that also produced the Enlightenment, clings doggedly to his conclusions, seeking out evidence that will support them. His conclusions, however, also involve some less obvious information. He knows, although readers still do not, of his lordship's total lack of sexual history, so he suspects that the presence of the whore Fanny may itself be a ruse to hide a homosexual affair between his lordship and the servant, Dick Thurlow. With nearly every subsequent witness the barrister pursues a line of questioning regarding untoward familiarity between master and servant, particularly (and this seems to horrify the class-conscious lawyer even more) whether the servant may have been the sexual master. He can envision few reasons for this unwarranted flight to the uncivilized southwest, and what he perceives as deviant sexuality, coupled with a desire to wound a noble parent, seems the most likely explanation.

None of the interviewees, however, confirms his suspicions with corroborating evidence. Ayscough's task is difficult because of the limits placed on him by the social system. He can hint at improprieties yet cannot spell them out. He occasionally intimates that the person he seeks is someone other than he pretended to be, yet the barrister cannot state plainly who he was. In his attempt to ferret out the truth, however dirty, without attaching any dirt to the noble family, Ayscough walks a very narrow path. Readers, of course, can piece together the numerous clues in ways that characters cannot, arriving at the conclusion that the mystery man came from the uppermost ranks of the nobility. We see, for instance, his letters to "Your Grace," which appellation indicates a duke or archbishop—and, while some of his oblique references to "His Lordship" having strayed from the path chosen by his noble father suggest the latter, evidence late in the novel (the other son is a marquis) indicates the former. The lawyer's task is doubly difficult because none of his sources can be trusted; he finds himself forced to consort with all forms of humanity which he despises—a Welshman, an actor, a bagnio owner, a prostitute, radical religious nonconformists. Ayscough, having reached the center of mainstream society, discovers its marginalized people, to his disgust. He has given his life to the proposition that English civilization is defined by Oxford and Cambridge, Canterbury Cathedral and Buckingham Palace, the Church of England, the monarchy and the aristocracy.

Social change, however, comes not from society's center but from its periphery, from its outlanders and outcasts. One of the novel's major themes is that societies do change and that the one described here will change, too. In fact, no modern reader could doubt it. The cultural landscape of the late twentieth century little resembles that of the early eighteenth. Ayscough believes deeply in *inequality,* in the class system as the only hope of order, in the nobility as the seat of all that is good and the masses as a source of danger and chaos. Already in his day the elements that would overthrow that view were coming into being, and a mere forty years later a new nation would come into being, in part by citing a "self-evident" truth: "that all men are created equal." That truth is hardly self-evident for Ayscough, whose bullying tactics grow out of his—and his society's—belief in the right of the aristocracy to govern the lower classes. He threatens and blusters not on the basis of law but, rather, on the basis of the personal power of his employer. Fowles suggests that the rise of dissenting religion and the rise of democratic ideals occurred at the same historical moment because they grow out of the same philosophical and social backgrounds. The particular form of dissent, Shakerism, on which he has focused, lingered only briefly on the world's religious stage, yet the equality and democracy it embraced have stayed on, all but obliterating the monarchies of Ayscough's day. Britain's own royal family exists in a purely ceremonial capacity, often seeming to do little more than feed the mills of tabloid journalism.

The novel, too, is a product of that democratization of Western society, as Fowles well knows. Often dismissed in the eighteenth century as an entertainment for the rabble, the novel has risen with the middle class and, ultimately, with the literate classes, as literacy has worked its way down the social scale. English poetry of the seventeenth and eighteenth centuries presumed a certain level and type of education—elite, tradition bound, classicist, and classist. The novel has been a great leveler among art forms, comparatively inexpensive and accessible, presuming little about readers' educational attainment or class affiliation. While Ayscough has more affinity with Alexander Pope than Henry Fielding, the future lies with *Tom Jones,* not *The Dunciad.*

Already at the time of *A Maggot,* the novel has made itself felt. Indeed, characters even mention prose fiction as analogous to their situation. Mr. Bartholomew's cryptic explanation of his quest to Francis Lacy involves such a comparison:

> It would be juster to say we were like personages in a tale or novel, that had no knowledge they were such; and thought ourselves most real, not seeing we were made of imperfect words and ideas, and to serve other ends, far different from what we supposed. We might imagine this great Author of all as such and such, in our own image, sometimes cruel, sometimes merciful, as we do our kings. Notwithstanding in truth we knew no more of Him and His ends than of what lay in the moon, or the next world. (144–45)

Readers will recognize Fowlesian slyness in this passage, for it is truer than Lacy can possibly imagine. Lacy conceives of this analogy on a theological or ontological level, as indeed Bartholomew intends it. Yet Bartholomew is himself the author of their current situation, constructing a plot of which his characters are ignorant (as characters inevitably are). Then, too, these two men *are* characters in a novel about which they know nothing, with an author of whom they know nothing. In *Vanity Fair* William Makepeace Thackeray demolishes the illusion of realism by insisting on his puppet-master metaphor for his own role vis-à-vis the novel: he controls the action by pulling the strings of his puppets. Fowles pushes readers to the edge of recognizing a similar relation between novelist and novel, without the overt or heavy-handed insistence of Thackeray's conceit. If the dominant concern of *The French Lieutenant's Woman* is the author's lack of control, the dominant concern of *A Maggot* is the characters' lack of awareness. No character can see the larger plan, the entire pattern. Even Ayscough, who in many ways is the surrogate reader, piecing together and deciphering the events, ultimately fails to understand his "novel" because he does not know that he, too, is a character in it. His view is necessarily limited, although he does not see those limitations.

In his attempt to "read" Bartholomew's disappearance Ayscough progresses through the persons who had seen him immediately prior to the fateful day. After Puddicombe and Dorcas Heller he briefly interviews Sampson Beckford, the parish curate who met with Lacy the night before the disappearance. Beckford provides little information, though it is significant. He describes Lacy exactly, down to the wart on his nose and his taking snuff. He rules out highwaymen as the solution, noting that travelers in the region are too poor to provide adequate booty. And, finally, it is he who first divines Ayscough's secret—that Bartholomew is actually a son of the nobility. While the barrister declines to confirm Beckford's suspicion, his manner says all that need be said. Beckford's appearance provides one other piece of information, but it is of no use to Ayscough: he provides a demonstration of the barrister's manner with a person of quality, so that readers can gauge his rudeness and peremptoriness with those he considers his social inferiors. Ayscough's pleasantries with Beckford contrast sharply with his open hostility toward Lacy, so that when he calls Lacy's wife a whore without fear of contradiction or physical threat (although he is physically dwarfed by the actor), the lawyer shows himself to be a bully.

Beckford's deposition is followed in the text by Ayscough's first letter to "Your Grace," dated 4 August. The purpose of the letter is threefold: to set the date (as do all the "primary" documents—letters, depositions, news clippings); to reveal the lawyer's beliefs and presuppositions, chiefly that his lordship (Bartholomew) is still alive; and to display the transformation from bullying inquisitor to hired toady. If his demeanor is that of a diminutive bulldog toward his witnesses, it is that of slavish lapdog toward his master. His obsequiousness fairly leaps off the page, as when he refers to the duchess as "[your] august consort, to whom I beg leave to present my humblest compliments" (99). Such phrases of cringing respect pepper his letters, marking him as someone who never forgets his place, either with his betters or his inferiors. Save Beckford, he never appears with anyone even remotely of his own station.

The first breakthrough in his investigation is the arrival and testimony of Francis Lacy, the actor who impersonates Bartholomew's uncle on the journey. At this point in the quest for truth, Lacy is the only person who can supply the missing elements without supplying everything. His knowledge, while limited, is key. Lacy has been paid the princely sum of 100 guineas for his performance during the journey and is able to supply details of his being hired. Further, he himself engaged David Jones, a Welshman, drunkard, and failed actor, for the part

of the strutting and boasting Farthing. He also supplies information about certain externals of the trip, specifically of a side trip
to Stonehenge which Bartholomew took, first in the daytime with
Lacy and a second time at night with Dick and Louise. This last
information, however, comes not directly but, instead, through
Jones and reveals Lacy's weakness as a witness: because of the
"Uncle's" station, he has little contact with the goings-on of the
group. Lacy is hired to be seen, not to see, and Bartholomew
keeps him in the dark as much as possible. Jones, sharing bed
space with Dick and acting as hired escort, is privy to much more,
although he too is frequently deceived.

When Lacy's examination resumes (having paused for the
deposition of Hannah Claiborne, Fanny's brothel keeper), he
moves from the journey to the last night, when Bartholomew
comes nearest to revealing his plan in full. Lacy is told that his
employer is "searching for his life's meridian" (165), and the
surveying metaphor—a meridian being the center line by which
land can be measured—suggests not merely a center but also a
means of measuring, or plotting out, his existence. Yet, when
Lacy attempts to pursue the implications of this statement, he
meets with riddles, mocking questions, apparent non sequiturs.
Ayscough can see no more in this than the continuance of a
perverse wasting of gifts and talents which have characterized his
lordship, waste that the lawyer ascribes not to mere filial misbe-
havior but "to Deviltry" (182).

The Devil plays an active role in the lives of the characters
of the novel. They believe in him, understand evil in terms of him,
see his agents in the world. Ayscough proves himself to be a hard
judge, utterly lacking in any feel for nuance, chiefly because of

his belief in Deviltry. The dichotomy between Heaven and Hell, God and Devil, leaves no room for subtlety. All this is in contrast to his creator, for Fowles sees evil as a human construct, even as a human failing to properly understand or do good. In his work evil is sometimes a product of malice, but more often it results from ineptitude or failure of will. In this novel the presence of evil is problematic, for what appears to be a wholesale murder turns out to be nothing of the sort. Aside from Dick's suicide, and that stems from despair or incomprehension, there is no provable evil. His lordship's disappearance ultimately resembles that of Elijah, swept away to another world. Lacy and Jones are demonstrably better off in financial terms, while Rebecca is reconciled with her family, rescued from Claiborne's bagnio, and turned to a life that is far preferable to her London existence. Her child, moreover, will change the world, or at least some small part of it.

The evil, then, is a measure of the characters' perception rather than of achieved fact. One may fear or despise what one does not understand; that does not prove that it is either fearsome or despicable. In this novel, as in his others, Fowles presents a human world in which good and evil are equally attainable, in which narrow-mindedness and received ideas present as much threat to the general welfare as any demonic agency, in which moral choice is not only an option but a requirement. His lordship, Rebecca, Ayscough—all are presented with dilemmas of being, knowledge, and ethics, and all must make choices. Rebecca, formerly so fearful of Claiborne's power and her enforcers, could elect to go back to the brothel after her adventure. Rather, she chooses to return to her family, seek their forgiveness, and change her life. Ayscough's difficulties resemble those of Dostoyevsky's Grand Inquisitor: he is confronted with a reality he cannot accept, yet he is unable to reject it. In fact, Rebecca's last statement to him, her gift of "more love" (444), resembles no moment in literature more than Christ's kiss bestowed on the Inquisitor, and it troubles him nearly as much.

Before they can arrive at that moment, of course, she must be found, and to that end Jones must first be found, and he is. Jones's testimony is invaluable, since he is the first witness to what transpires after the party rides west on May Day morn. Having discovered Bartholomew's real identity, Jones disappears on the fateful morning only to spy on the party, stationing himself near a fork in the Bideford road, in hopes of gaining some reward from the irate noble father. Jones proves to be the most amusing narrator of the entire book, for his speech is a nearly unbroken string of similes and metaphors, only some of them apt, which have an infuriating effect on Ayscough. For example, when the trio arrives at the eventual site the young woman is given the dress of a May Queen and must make her crown: "She made her maying crown, and looked as innocent there amidst the green as a pail of milk. Faith, she'd have slain a blind man, as 'tis said. She was killing pretty dressed so, spite of all" (219). Jones's barrage of figurative language allows Ayscough frequent recourse to sarcasm, for Jones is so unaware of his verbal mannerisms that he provides a perfect foil to the very canny barrister.

As a direct witness, Jones is limited. He follows the trio up a cwm, his Welsh word for a steep hollow or ravine, away from the road to a cavern, in front of which stands a tall stone on end, like those at Stonehenge but shorter. This is the place where Louise changes into her May costume. Bartholomew, Dick, and

Louise are then received by a woman in a silver outfit, which is
decribed like a space suit, before whom they kneel. From here
Jones's information is sketchy. They follow the woman into the
cave, Dick and Louise walking hand in hand "like as they are
some man and bride before the church rails on their wedding-day"
(223). Louise falls to her knees and begs, presumably not to go on,
and Bartholomew draws his sword to force her in. Once they
enter Jones notes nothing except a faint smoke and hum coming
from the cave, until Dick and Louise emerge hours later, Dick
running in terror, Louise naked and in a daze, again falling to her
knees. She seems not injured but, rather, "planet-struck," in
Jones's opinion. Of actual events he knows no more and must
wait until after dinner to recount the story Louise has told him. In
the interval a narrative section focuses on Ayscough's time alone
with his private thoughts, including views on property rights,
criminal law, Conformist Anglicanism, and Conservatism. It is a
telling portrait, and Fowles pauses to tell us, as he has done in *The
French Lieutenant's Woman,* that Ayscough's world is nearly
done, that Jones, as a member of the despised rabble, represents
the egalitarian future confronting Ayscough's hidebound elitist
past. Characters are never aware of such niceties, of course, and
the barrister is too intent on his victim's story to reflect on this
matter, even were he capable of seeing it.

Jones's tale fits in perfectly with a worldview that sees an
active role for Satan, so perfectly, in fact, that readers may rightly
suspect it as a fabrication. Louise tells him a story of witchcraft
and satanic possession, beginning with the episode at Stonehenge.
There she is made to lie on a stone slab, presumably to cure
Bartholomew's complaint, while a "blackamoor," a dark-skinned

person, appears out of a gust of air, hovering over her then disappearing in the same manner, leaving a hot stench. All of these elements play into the iconography of Hell—the blackness, the night, the brimstone-like odor, the sudden appearance—so that she need not identify them but can, instead, rely on Jones's religious imagination to interpret them.

In the cave the Silver Lady proves to be malevolent, and, joined by two others, she recalls the three witches from *Macbeth.* Shakespeare, naturally enough, drew on popular beliefs and tales for his work, so it is unsurprising that Louise should come up with the same number, particularly in light of superstition related to numbers. The three form an obscene parody of the Trinity. A hangman is also present, whom she identifies as Satan, again a blackamoor, this time with fiery red eyes. He performs a marriage between his lordship and the youngest hag (both naked) then permits them to kiss his genitals, setting off an orgy among the group. Even here Ayscough attempts to find evidence of homosexual involvement between his lordship and Dick Thurlow. With the help of the hags Satan then rapes Rebecca (as Jones now calls her, the shift suggesting that a change in her character has already taken place), who has first swooned and then been given a drugged potion to make her sleep. Upon waking, Rebecca is treated to a host of terrifying scenes, with the Devil playing the part of projectionist or stage manager: a beggar girl who cries out but melts in flame before Rebecca can save her, Rebecca's parents with a carpenter (presumably Christ) standing close but unreachable, and, finally, a female corpse being eaten by maggots. This last is Jones's explanation for her phrase "the maggot, the maggot" uttered upon first waking from her faint outside the cave. The phrase echoes Conrad's "the horror, the horror" and is equally cryptic and central. She also tells of a huge spinning wheel as the source of the smoke Jones sees coming from the cave. This image recalls Ezekiel's wheel and, as with all the images in her tale, is fairly predictable and recognizable in terms of sources and traditions. It also suggests that something she cannot explain is indeed present in the cave, although what that thing is must wait for explanation. Ayscough, naturally enough, has some problems believing this account. Why does Satan not take her, such an obvious case for damnation? Why would she swear to know no more men carnally? And, more to the point, why should he believe that? Why does she claim to be saved? Yet the basic imagery of the story troubles him not at all, since it all comes from the common stock of religious and popular symbols.

Jones's testimony having come to an end, Fowles breaks the pace of the narrative with a series of letters, first from Ayscough to his employer then from attorney Richard Pygge to Ayscough. Pygge has been conducting research for Ayscough and provides background on Rebecca's family, Quakers in Bristol called Hocknell, and on the cave. There is a Faustian story of a shepherd, his son, and the Devil associated with the cave, and the upright stone is therefore known as Devil's Stone. The ashes in the cave he explains as coming from Gypsies, although he does note a smell of sulphur or vitriol. The baked earth outside the cave gives evidence of a huge fire, although there is no sign of ashes, nor is such a fire customary with the secretive Gypsies. Ultimately, Pygge supplies eight points of evidence, the cumulative effect of which is contradictory and confusing. He believes Dick to have been hanged by thieves, chiefly because the horses and chest have disappeared. There is an obscure path across Exmoor by which his lordship could have escaped, which becomes Ayscough's one small point of hope he can give to the family. Additionally, no sign of other new graves has shown up. There are no known covens of witches in the area, nor is the location noted for miracle cures, so comparatively few of the particulars of Jones's tale fit the locale. Pygge also sends along a sample of the baked earth, which a scientific expert cannot identify. The letters solve the age-old problem of introducing exposition into a novel, particularly one that rests so heavily on dialogue. They also break the rhythm of question and answer, which threatens to become oppressive after a certain time. Fowles is clearly aware of the pitfalls of his narrative method and works brilliantly to avoid them.

Finally, five months after the event, the fugitive female is discovered. Ayscough's wording to the duke, "She we seek is found," recalls Montague's letter to Charles regarding Sarah in *The French Lieutenant's Woman*, and, indeed, the two are quite similar. Like Sarah, Rebecca proves to be a difficult witness, supplying information at her will rather than that of the questioner, contradicting a social superior, manifesting a silent stubbornness that infuriates the male aggressor. As Carol Barnum asserts, Rebecca shares with Sarah the willing acceptance of "the persona of outcast to have the freedom to create a different life."[3]

Under questioning, she gives a completely different version than she has given Jones. Her reasoning is that he would not understand the truth, and the version she tells him virtually guarantees his silence. Such thinking displays her shrewd judgment of human nature. Her story from the nocturnal visit to Stonehenge involves some of the same elements, the rushing noise as of wind, for instance, but their effect is divine rather than demonic. There is a great light suspended in the sky and a sweet, rather than an acrid, smell. Additionally, there are two male figures, distinctly nonthreatening, and her fear leaves her. Similarly, their arrival at the cave differs from the outset. She is made to bathe before putting on her new, virginal costume, so that she will have, as she puts it, "no taint of my former world on me" (343); the parallel to baptism, washing away previous sins to take on a new identity, is clear. With each contradiction to Jones's version the barrister tries to trick her out, yet she proves unflappable, saying she knowingly lied to Jones. She will not be shaken in her current story.

Throughout her narrative readers are reminded that she and Ayscough lack the vocabulary to describe the experience, just as they lack the vocabulary to understand each other properly. One of Rebecca's constant refrains is that she cannot tell him "in thy alphabet," reminding readers that something completely outside one's experience cannot be comprehended. Three women do appear—young, prime, and elderly—differing only by the flowers they carry, then melt into the middle one. Their appearance suggests the Trinity yet not in the openly blasphemous way of her account to Jones. Rather, it explains her later insistence (and that of her famous daughter, Ann Lee) on the inclusion of the female in the Godhead. After sharing a fruit drink, implying both nectar of the gods and communion, they watch scenes displayed on a telescreen, another unexplainable miracle.

What she sees on this screen is a vision of paradise, and its elements are those that ultimately appear in Shakerism—simplicity, agrarianism, celibacy, communal and communistic living, pacifism. She sees a man with a scythe who is not the grim reaper but, instead, Christ. The woman who leads them is Holy Mother Wisdom, the Edenic paradise June Eternal, both of which ideas Ayscough finds blasphemous. The video display then turns to the horrors of modern warfare, with tanks and bombers, as well as a host of crimes and sins. When the showing is done, his lordship, now dressed in silver as well, issues a laughably unnecessary injunction, "Forget me not, Rebecca" (386); how could she forget such an experience, even if she wished to?

After an interruption by the contentious males in her life and her religious sect, Ayscough and Rebecca focus on her understanding of these strange events. She claims her child will bring "more light and more love" (424) and asserts that his lordship was lord in a world beyond this one. She believes he was the spiritual side, Dick the physical side, of a united pair, and that, the spirit having flown, the corporeal self must die. Further, she asserts that his lordship is the true father of her child "of the spirit, not the seed" (433). Once more this reference comes just close enough to standard Christian teaching, in this case the virgin birth, to infuriate Ayscough, as does her assertion that standard religious thinking is false because it presents only the male point of view. The interview comes to an abrupt standstill when she sees his lordship in his new guise standing in the corner of the world. Of course, Ayscough, the rationalist and empiricist, can see nothing and suspects a trick. Afterward she begins sobbing. With the appearance of his lordship, the investigation is effectively finished. It remains only for the two to trade pleasantries. Ayscough gives her a prophecy, that she will be hanged yet; Rebecca, in a final infuriating gesture, gives him "more love" in the manner of her sect's greetings and farewells (444), yet it is more than a mere formula.

In his final letter to the duke, Ayscough confesses a certain amount of failure, knowing by now that he will never reach the truth of the affair. He suspects that his lordship is probably destroyed by whatever scheme he has concocted to stir up sedition and that, "hoist on his own petard" (showing that even a despiser of the theater can quote Shakespeare), he commits suicide, with Dick following suit from despair at being deserted. He can only surmise that his lordship made the scenes in the cave appear by magic. The barrister, loyal family retainer to the end, does hold out the possibility that his lordship escaped to some unknown place; this unlikelihood is offered chiefly as a sop to the bereaved mother and is presented as such.

The narrative does not end with Ayscough, however. Fowles is canny enough to know that mysterious pregnancies must be brought to term and that readers will want to see the promised infant, so he closes with the birth scene. In a sense all birth scenes close out the adult males in the environment, yet this one particularly excludes them. Rebecca, headstrong to the end, rejects John Lee's choice of a name for her daughter. Lee remains the perpetual outsider, as removed at birth as he is at conception. Rebecca insists again that the Redeemer's next coming will be as a woman, and she wins out in the matter of naming. The final image, of Rebecca suckling Ann, presents a scene that categorically excludes the male. Rebecca's world is one of feeling and spirit, rather than reason and mind; for her, truth is a sensory rather than a rational issue, of being rather than of knowing.

Ayscough, on the other hand, represents almost pure mind. He is almost all mind; much is made in the narrative of his tiny physique, as if his corporeal self scarcely exists. Similarly, the spirit side hardly makes an impact, and what shakes him about Rebecca is her near total reliance on spirit and emotion. Like many rationalists, Ayscough violates his precepts by arriving at his conclusions in advance of the facts, causing him to overlook or even misconstrue key testimony that is presented to him. Yet for all his determination he shows at the end that his conviction that logic can penetrate mystery is shakable. Indeed, his major crisis is the failure of logic and reason in the face of mystery, miracle, and faith. He must reject Rebecca's experience in the cave, but he fails utterly to make her also reject it and to arrive at some truth he can find plausible. The novel explores the relation between reason and unreason, what the great Argentine writer Jorge Luis Borges called *irrealidad:* the irreal, the uncanny, the magical or fantastic.

This, too, is the crisis for the novel after realism: How can a mode of fiction best suited to capturing the quotidian, the average, be made to accommodate the uncanny, without relegating it to some demeaned category of fable, fantasy, tale? Ayscough, while not a literary creator, represents the turn of mind that led to literary realism being the favored mode for more than a century. Fowles is the literary creator who seeks to work in the realistic tradition without being dominated by it. His struggle, like that of his great contemporary Gabriel García Márquez, involves his attempt to account for the uncanny, the numinous, while working within a tradition designed to reveal the everyday, the phenomenal.

Readers, too, may be trapped in their own versions of rationalism and cozy worldviews. Readers may smile at Jones's credulity at Rebecca's first story, yet who can say they are not gulled in their turn? As Katherine Tarbox notes, "From the

UNDERSTANDING JOHN FOWLES

beginning Fowles defines the limits and weaknesses of ordinary perception,"[4] and those deficiencies extend to readers as well. The fact that modern readers recognize the elements of her tale does not guarantee its veracity. Ayscough may be right to doubt her, or she may be telling the absolute truth. There is no way of determining, and ultimately readers must choose for themselves, knowing there is an element of risk involved in choice.

Fowles closes the novel with an epilogue, in which he reveals the somewhat tenuous connection to Shakerism which his book has and in which he reveals a surprising affinity for this strangest of Christian sects. Some of his appreciation is coy, as when he says that Shakerism and the novel both require an immense metaphorical understanding to find the "truths behind our tropes" (463). More to the point, he pinpoints the birth of the modern sense of Self from the founding of such movements as Ann Lee's Shakerism and John Wesley's Methodism. The rise of Dissenting Protestantism, with its emphasis on the individual believer, coincides with the rise of the democratic ideal, with its emphasis on the individual citizen. If *A Maggot* is Fowles's least overtly existentialist novel, it is nevertheless the work that examines the historical framework that ultimately makes existentialism, with its total emphasis on the individual, possible. He also cites our need to escape "mere science, mere reason," and to heed Ann's appeal for "simplicity, sanity and self-control" (465). Ever the difficult citizen, he claims in closing that "dissent . . . is, I suspect, our most precious legacy to the world" (466). Readers who see the epilogue as a paean to Shakerism are likely to be angered by the seemingly unwarranted intrusion on the narrative of extraneous elements, yet the closing stands as a necessary component of the text, underscoring the philosophical elements that may well become lost in the mass of detail and maze of narrative. The novel calls for vision, spirit, and moral courage, for simplicity and personal wholeness, elements an avowed atheist can share with the strongest of individualist Christians. These are aspects of the human condition Fowles has explored throughout his career, and, if *A Maggot* brings them together in a new way, they nevertheless remain recognizable and essential parts of his vision.

Notes

1. John Fowles, *A Maggot* (Boston: Little, Brown, 1985) 1. Subsequent references will be noted parenthetically.

2. Wallace Stevens, *The Collected Poems of Wallace Stevens* (New York: Knopf, 1977) 203.

3. Carol M. Barnum, *The Fiction of John Fowles* (Greenwood, Fla.: Penkeville, 1988) 142.

4. Katherine Tarbox, *The Art of John Fowles* (Athens: U of Georgia P, 1988) 136.

Conclusion

The career of John Fowles has resembled, more than any other, that of Thomas Hardy. Like Hardy, he moved to the southwest of England to pursue his craft. There, far from the madding crowd, he created fiction of the individual in conflict with the world, of the outcast and the misfit trying to find a place in the universe. Like Hardy, his writing celebrates the local, the rural, the natural—the old green England. Like Hardy, he has sought meaning in a world devoid of God, or in which God is hostile or indifferent. In pursuing a highly personal vision, he has asked universal theological and existential questions. And, finally, like Hardy, his fame and importance have spread from a corner of Dorset to a much larger arena.

In the range and depth of his work John Fowles has shown himself to be not merely one of the leading contemporary practitioners of the novel but a major theorist of the novel as well. His experiments with fictional form have put him at the forefront of current novelists. To a large degree his continuing critical and popular success has rested on his ability to combine metafictional strategies with the structures of traditional narrative. He has recognized the very considerable pleasures readers take from the conventional novel, the emotional and aesthetic pleasures provided by Dickens, Fielding, and Hardy. At the same time, he has sought, in the manner of Sterne and Joyce, to extend the range of the novel, to find new possibilities in an old form. That he has been able to find a large readership for his always challenging, often lengthy work in an age of thirty-minute television programs is testimony to the human appeal of that work. His novels are not cold clinical experiments; rather, they are, like Conchis's godgame, plots that draw readers into the action and involve them intellectually, emotionally, and morally.

Indeed, one of the major satisfactions of a Fowles novel is its appeal to the intellect. Whether it is the multiple endings and authorial appearances of *The French Lieutenant's Woman* or the machinations of Conchis in *The Magus,* the mysterious visitation in *A Maggot* or the mysterious disappearance in "The Enigma," Fowles's fiction requires and rewards thought and consideration. At the same time, he does not limit the appeal of his work to the joys of intellection. Gamesmanship and brilliance alone are insufficient to carry readers' interest for the long run. Instead, he also involves readers in the fates of his characters, giving us characters whose lives matter to us. Sarah Woodruff is as mysterious to a contemporary audience as she is to Charles Smithson, and one finds oneself passionately drawn into what becomes of the two characters even before Fowles makes one choose an ending for their story.

Along with the intellectual and emotional appeal of his work, Fowles includes a powerful moral vision. The choices his characters make, and the choices his readers must also make, carry a strong ethical component. He is like his compatriot Iris

Murdoch in his philosophical interests, investigating existence and identity, knowledge and the experience of time, the nature of love, and issues of morality and conduct. A Fowles novel typically explores how men and women treat one another in a world in which the old verities of religion and society seem no longer to obtain. His protagonists struggle to become complete human beings, capable of understanding themselves and caring about someone other than themselves. If they do not uniformly succeed, they at least have the opportunity, and readers can learn as much from their failures as from their successes. The novels, like the godgame, are laboratories for the study of human ethical conduct, asking, in effect, can this person be saved, can this deficient character become emotionally and morally whole? The opening sentence to *Daniel Martin,* "Whole sight, or all the rest is desolation," could stand as an epigraph to the Fowles canon. Like Thomas Hardy, Fowles is passionately interested in, and invites readers to be interested in, human beings in their entirety. Like his great predecessor, he knows there is no better subject for fiction.

BIBLIOGRAPHY

Works by John Fowles

Fiction

The Collector. London: Jonathan Cape, 1963; Boston: Little, Brown, 1963.

Daniel Martin. London: Jonathan Cape, 1977; Boston: Little, Brown, 1977.

The Ebony Tower. London: Jonathan Cape, 1974; Boston: Little, Brown, 1974.

The French Lieutenant's Woman. London: Jonathan Cape, 1969; Boston: Little, Brown, 1969.

A Maggot. London: Jonathan Cape, 1985; Boston: Little, Brown, 1985.

The Magus. London: Jonathan Cape, 1966; Boston: Little, Brown, 1965.

The Magus: A Revised Version. London: Jonathan Cape, 1977; Boston: Little, Brown, 1978.

Mantissa. London: Jonathan Cape, 1982; Boston: Little, Brown, 1982.

Selected Nonfiction

The Aristos. London: Jonathan Cape, 1964; Boston: Little, Brown, 1964. Rev. ed., 1970.

A Brief History of Lyme. Lyme Regis, U.K.: Friends of the Museum, 1985.

The Enigma of Stonehenge. Cowritten by Barry Brukoff. New York: Summit, 1980.

Islands. Photographs by Fay Godwin. Boston: Little, Brown, 1979.

Lyme Regis: Three Town Walks. Lyme Regis, U.K.: Friends of the Lyme Regis Museum, 1983.

Medieval Lyme Regis. Lyme Regis, U.K.: Lyme Regis (Philpot) Museum, 1984.

BIBLIOGRAPHY

Of Memoirs and Magpies. Austin, Tex.: Taylor, 1983.
Poems. New York: Ecco, 1973.
Shipwreck. Photographs by the Gibsons of Scilly. London: Jonathan Cape, 1975; Boston: Little, Brown, 1975.
A Short History of Lyme Regis. Boston: Little, Brown, 1982.
The Tree. Photographs by Frank Horvat. New York: Ecco, 1983.

Selected Essays

Afterword. *The Lost Domain (Le Grand meaulnes).* By Henri Alain-Fournier. Trans. Frank Davison. Oxford UP, 1986. Published as *The Wanderer, or The End of Youth.* New York: NAL, 1971.
"The Falklands, and a Death Foretold." *Georgia Review* 36 (1982):721–28.
Foreword. *The Screenplay of The French Lieutenant's Woman.* By Harold Pinter and Karel Reisz. Boston: Little, Brown, 1981.
Foreword. *The Lais of Marie de France.* Trans. Robert Hanning and Joan Ferrante. New York: Dutton, 1978.
Foreword and afterword. *The Hound of the Baskervilles.* By Arthur Conan Doyle. London: Murray, 1974.
"Hardy and the Hag." *Thomas Hardy After Fifty Years.* Ed. Lance St. John Butler. Totowa, N.J.: Rowman, 1977. 28–42.
Introduction. *Miramar.* By Naguib Mahfouz. Cairo: Heinemann, 1978; New York: Book of the Month Club, 1989.
Introduction, glossary, and appendix. *Mehalah: A Story of the Salt Marshes.* By S. Baring-Gould. London: Chatto, 1969.
"I Write Therefore I Am." *Evergreen Review* 8 (Aug.–Sept. 1964): 16–17, 89–90.
"Making a Pitch for Cricket." *Sports Illustrated,* 21 May 1973, 100–103, 106, 108, 111–12, 115–16. Reprinted as "Baseball's Other Self: Cricket." *A Baseball Album.* Ed. Gerald Secor Couzens. New York: Lippincott, 1980. 21–24, 26–33, 35–36.

BIBLIOGRAPHY

"Notes on an Unfinished Novel." *Afterwords: Novelists on Their Novels.* Ed. Thomas McCormack. New York: Harper, 1969.
"When the Bug Bites—Write." *London Times,* 12 October 1985, 8.

Translations

Cinderella. By Charles Perrault. London: Jonathan Cape, 1974.
Ourika. By Claire de Durfort. Austin, Tex.: Taylor, 1977.
Don Juan. By Molière. Dir. Peter Gill. National Theatre Company, 7 April 1981.
Lorenzaccio. By Alfred de Musset. Dir. Michael Bogdanov. National Theatre Company, 15 March 1981.
Martine. By Jean-Jacques Bernard. Dir. Peter Hall. National Theatre Company, 20 April 1985.

Interviews

Baker, James R. "The Art of Fiction CIX: John Fowles." *Paris Review* 111 (1989): 40–63.
———. "An Interview with John Fowles." *Michigan Quarterly Review* 25 (1986): 661–83.
Barber, Michael. *An Interview with John Fowles.* Audio-text cassette no. 38873. N. Hollywood, Calif.: Center for Cassette Studies, 1979.
Barnum, Carol M. "An Interview with John Fowles." *Modern Fiction Studies* 31 (1985): 187–203.
Campbell, James. "An Interview with John Fowles." *Contemporary Literature* 17 (1976): 455–69.
Foulke, Robert. "A Conversation with John Fowles." *Salmagundi* 68–69 (1985–1986): 367–84.
Gussow, Mel. "Talk with John Fowles." *New York Times Book Review,* 13 November 1977, 3, 84–85.

BIBLIOGRAPHY

North, David. "Interview with John Fowles." *Macleans,* 14 November 1977, 4, 6, 8.

Robinson, Robert. "Giving the Reader a Choice—A Conversation with John Fowles." *Listener,* 31 October 1974, 584.

Romano, Carlin. "A Conversation with John Fowles." *Boulevard* (Spring 1987): 37–52.

Singh, Raman K. "An Encounter with John Fowles." *Journal of Modern Literature* 8 (1980–1981): 181–202.

Works about John Fowles

Books

Aubrey, James R. *John Fowles: A Reference Companion.* New York: Greenwood, 1991. A sourcebook on Fowles's life and fiction, with a lengthy, useful biographical chapter. The annotations to the novels are particularly helpful. Contains a primary and selected secondary bibliography.

Barnum, Carol M. *The Fiction of John Fowles: A Myth for Our Time.* Greenwood, Fla.: Penkeville, 1988. Explores the Jungian psychological thinking and imagery of Fowles's work, seeing the result as a unified body of personal myth.

Cooper, Pamela. *The Fictions of John Fowles: Power, Creativity, Femininity.* Ottawa: U of Ottawa P, 1991. A deconstructive reading that explores issues of gender, freedom, and power, finding that Fowles's efforts inevitably set up his women as victims of male power (including male authorial power).

Fawkner, H. W. *The Timescapes of John Fowles.* Rutherford, N.J.: Fairleigh Dickinson UP, 1984. A comprehensive investigation of the uses of time in Fowles's novels.

BIBLIOGRAPHY

Kane, Richard C. *Iris Murdoch, Muriel Spark, and John Fowles: Didactic Demons in Modern Fiction.* Rutherford, N.J.: Fairleigh Dickinson UP, 1988. Examines the way all three writers use the demonic as a means of ethical investigation.

Loveday, Simon. *The Romances of John Fowles.* New York: St. Martin's, 1985. Considers Fowles as a romancer with realistic tendencies.

Neary, John. *Something and Nothingness: The Fiction of John Updike and John Fowles.* Carbondale: Southern Illinois UP, 1992. Discusses Fowles as following a "negative way," based on Sartre, which informs his deconstructive, metafictionist tendencies, while Updike follows a more Kierkegaardian "positive way," which leads him more toward social realism and Christian affirmation.

Palmer, William J. *The Fiction of John Fowles: Tradition, Art, and the Loneliness of Selfhood.* Columbia: U of Missouri P, 1974. An early monograph focusing on Fowles's relation to the realistic tradition, on his views of art and pornography, and on his use of existentialist isolation and alienation.

Pilfer, Ellen, ed. *Critical Essays on John Fowles.* Boston: G. K. Hall, 1986. Essays from a variety of critics and writers, including the author himself.

Runyon, Randolph. *Fowles/Irving/Barthes: Canonical Variations on and Apocryphal Theme.* Oxford, Ohio: Miami UP and Ohio State UP, 1981. Explores these writers in terms of a common theme drawn from the Book of Tobit in the Old Testament Apocrypha.

Salami, Mahmoud. *John Fowles's Fiction and the Poetics of Postmodernism.* Rutherford, N.J.: Fairleigh Dickinson UP, 1992. Discusses Fowles's work as a warehouse of postmodern narrative concerns: intertextuality, unreliability, self-reflexivity, dialogism, gender and power issues, and imprisonment and seduction.

Tarbox, Katherine. *The Art of John Fowles.* Athens: U of Georgia P, 1988. Treats the major novels as elaborations on the themes of time, freedom, morality, and narrative technique adumbrated in *The Magus.*

BIBLIOGRAPHY

Wolfe, Peter. *John Fowles: Magus and Moralist.* Lewisburg, Pa.: Bucknell UP, 1976. Rev. ed., 1979. Discusses the novels in terms of how Fowles uses his narrative magic to pursue his ethical concerns. Chapters on *The Aristos* and each of the first three novels. The revised version includes a chapter on *Daniel Martin* but omits, curiously, *The Ebony Tower.*

Woodcock, Bruce. *Male Mythologies: John Fowles and Masculinity.* Sussex: Harvester; Totowa, N.J.: Barnes, 1984. Examines Fowles's use of "masculine ideology," especially the way he presents male characters who are full of standard male deficiencies as a means of exploring sexual myths.

Critical Articles

Bradbury, Malcolm. "The Novelist as Impresario: The Fiction of John Fowles." *No, Not Bloomsbury.* New York: Columbia UP, 1988, 279–93. Fowles is a novelist who frees the traditional novel from its notions of formal regularity and verisimilitude through his insistence on freedom, magic, the erotic, and the enigmatic. He is both a traditional virtuoso and a metafictional experimentalist.

Davidson, Arnold E. "The Barthesian Configuration of John Fowles's 'The Cloud.'" *Centennial Review* 28, no. 4–29, no. 1 (1984–1985): 80–93. Asserts that Fowles shares with Roland Barthes's *Mythologies* a critique of bourgeois culture and that he has moved from existentialism to structuralism in a story of codes, games, dialectic pairings, and embedded tales.

Eddins, Dwight. "John Fowles: Existence as Authorship." *Contemporary Literature* 17 (1976): 204–22. Discusses the first three novels as metafictions, examining the "problem of fictiveness" for characters who become, in a sense, their own authors.

BIBLIOGRAPHY

Haegert, John. "Memoirs of a Deconstructive Angel: The Heroine as Mantissa in the Fiction of John Fowles." *Contemporary Literature* 27 (1986): 160–81. Argues that *Mantissa* recognizes the authorial anxiety of underestimating the mystery and "colossal subversiveness" of the author's creative imagination. Fowles's response to this anxiety is to move his "female principle" from a mortal woman into his own imagination, changing her/it from a catalyst to a prime mover of his work.

Hill, Roy Mack. "Power and Hazard: John Fowles's Theory of Play." *Journal of Modern Literature* 8 (1980–1981): 211–18. John Fowles special number. Associates Fowles's use of play with Johan Huizanga's theories in *Homo Ludens: A Study of the Play Element in Culture* (1950), finding that games in the novels represent chance, hazard, and freedom operating within fixed limits.

Lewis, Janet E., and Barry N. Olshen. "John Fowles and the Medieval Romance Tradition." *Modern Fiction Studies* 31 (1985): 15–30. John Fowles special number. Discusses medieval courtly romance not as a mere series of allusions in the novels but, rather, as a continuing informing influence on the actions of characters and the structure of the fiction.

McDaniel, Ellen. "Games and Godgames in *The Magus* and *The French Lieutenant's Woman*." *Modern Fiction Studies* 31 (1985): 31–42. Argues that Fowles uses his novels as Conchis and Sarah use their games, parables, and riddles: as transparently fictional devices that manipulate in order to teach. Games—and novels—replace life and create small worlds in which "absolute order reigns."

McSweeney, Kerry. "Withering into Truth: John Fowles and *Daniel Martin*." *Critical Quarterly* 20, no. 4 (1978): 31–38. An assessment of the weaknesses and strengths of *Daniel Martin*, with a view to placing it within the Fowles canon. McSweeney feels that there is too much discrepancy between the "thematic strength and the felt weakness of its two main characters."

BIBLIOGRAPHY

Olshen, Barry N. "John Fowles's *The Magus*: An Allegory of Self-Realization." *Journal of Popular Culture* 9 (1976): 916–25. Sees the novel as an allegory of everyman's search for self-realization, drawing on "four different models of experience: from mythology, psychology, philosophy, and mysticism."

Bibliographies

Dixon, Ronald C. "Criticism of John Fowles: A Selected Checklist." *Modern Fiction Studies* 31 (1985): 205–10. Secondary.

Evarts, Prescott, Jr. "John Fowles: A Checklist." *Critique* 13, no. 3 (1972): 105–7. Primary and secondary.

Myers, Karen Magee. "John Fowles: An Annotated Bibliography, 1963–1976." *Bulletin of Bibliography* 32, no. 3 (1976): 162–69. Primary and secondary.

Olshen, Barry N., and Toni A. Olshen. *John Fowles: A Reference Guide.* Boston: Hall, 1980. Primary and secondary.

Roberts, Ray A. "John Fowles: A Bibliographical Checklist." *American Book Collector* 1, no. 5 (1980): 26–37. Primary.

INDEX

Alain-Fournier, Henri
  Le Grand Meaulnes, 15, 62
Arthurian legend, 10
Austen, Jane
  Emma, 27

Bakhtin, Mikhail, 16–17
Barnum, Carol, 25, 59, 96, 106, 161
Barth, John, 16, 67
Barthes, Roland, 15, 84, 109
Beauvoir, Simone de, 36
Beckett, Samuel, 36, 40, 124
Bentham, Jeremy, 68
Bergman, Ingmar, 124
Borges, Jorge Luis, 16, 17, 67, 88, 165
Bretonne, Restif de la
  Monsieur Nicolas 124
Buber, Martin, 5
Bulwer-Lytton, Edward, 86
Buñuel, Luis, 124
Burgess, Anthony
  A Clockwork Orange, 21–22
Burne-Jones, Edward, 74
Byatt, A. S., 67
Byron, George Gordon, Lord, 42, 70, 124

Calvino, Italo, 16, 67, 111, 141
Camus, Albert, 5, 8, 36, 40, 42, 43, 72, 73
  The Myth of Sisyphus, 36–37, 72
  The Plague, 43
Carroll, Lewis
  Alice in Wonderland, 104

INDEX

Chaucer, Geoffrey
  "The Miller's Tale," 61
Chrétien de Troyes, 15, 93
Christie, Agatha, 103
Coleridge, Samuel Taylor
  Biographia Literaria, 84
Conrad, Joseph
  Heart of Darkness, 160
Cooper, Pamela, 13–14, 35, 111, 114
Coover, Robert, 16, 111, 141

Darwin, Charles, 73
Davies, Robertson, 67
  What's Bred in the Bone, 97–98
Dickens, Charles, 69, 70, 73, 169
  David Copperfield, 83
  Great Expectations, 62, 64, 73, 86
  The Pickwick Papers, 83
Dostoyevsky, Fyodor
  The Brothers Karamazov, 157
Durrell, Lawrence
  The Alexandria Quartet, 42

Eliot, George, 15, 73, 83
  Adam Bede, 84
Eliot, T. S.
  The Waste Land, 106, 109
Existentialism, 5, 8, 36–37, 39–40, 43, 72

Fielding, Henry, 169
  Tom Jones, 104, 152

INDEX

Fowles, John
    Atheism, 4, 146, 156, 167
    Childhood, 1–2
    Education, 2
    Hobbies, 2, 4
    Humanism, 5
    Life at Lyme Regis, Dorset, 3, 168
    Military service, 2
    Teaching career, 2–3
Works:
    Absurdity ("the nemo") in, 6–8, 36, 43
    Alienation in, 5–8, 36, 42–43
    The Aristos, 4, 5–6, 7, 9, 39, 42, 76, 98
    "The Cloud," 7–8, 102, 106–11
    The Collector, 2, 3, 4, 9, 12–13, 14, 20–37, 38–39, 115, 131, 147
    Daniel Martin, 1–2, 9, 11, 14, 17, 27, 108, 114, 119–39, 170
    The Ebony Tower, 11, 15, 91–111
    "The Ebony Tower," 13, 14, 15, 20, 35, 47, 75, 91–98, 102, 108, 115, 135
    "The Enigma," 6, 7, 102–6, 110, 140, 169
    Existentialism in, 42–44, 72–73, 105, 126, 166, 168
    Freedom in, 7–10, 54
    The French Lieutenant's Woman, 3, 5, 6, 7, 8, 9, 10–11, 13, 14, 17, 20, 47, 64, 67–90, 102, 110, 113, 116, 119, 132, 135, 136, 144–45, 153, 158, 161, 169
    Holocaust and Nazi images in, 36, 40, 45, 52–54
    Lyme Regis: Three Town Walks, 3
    A Maggot, 3, 4, 7, 11, 13, 14, 17, 31, 47, 140–67, 169
    The Magus, 2, 5, 6, 7, 9–10, 11, 13, 14, 17, 20, 31, 38–66, 75, 92, 97, 102, 108, 110, 116, 119, 120, 124, 132, 134, 135, 136, 137, 140, 141, 147, 169–70

INDEX

Fowles, John
    Works (continued)
Mantissa, 15, 17, 31, 47, 91, 111–18
    Medieval Lyme Regis, 3
    "Notes on an Unfinished Novel," 69, 73
    The Other in, 11–13, 31–33, 49, 74, 135
    "Poor Koko," 6, 91, 98–102
    Postmodernism in, 14, 83–89, 112–17, 120–21, 123–25, 140–42,
        168–69
    Quest myths in, 24–26, 47, 94–96, 105
    A Short History of Lyme, 3
    Traditionalism in, 14
    Treatment of women in, 13–14, 46–47, 49, 77–83, 132–33
    World War I in, 45
Forster, E. M.
    Howards End, 28, 131
Frank, Anne, 36
French Resistance (WWII), 36, 40
Frost, Robert, 119

Gass, William, 15–16
    Fiction and the Figures of Life, 16
    Habitations of the Word, 88
Gramsci, Antonio, 124

Hammett, Dashiell, 140
Hardy, Thomas, 15, 28, 69, 83, 121, 124, 168, 170
    Tess of the D'Urbervilles, 71, 73, 122
    Jude the Obscure, 73
Hawkes, John, 16

Heidegger, Martin, 5
Homer
 The Odyssey, 113
Huffaker, Robert, 120
Ionesco, Eugène
 Rhinoceros, 36

James, Henry, 124
 The Turn of the Screw, 62, 64
James, P. D., 103
Joyce, James, 169
 Finnegans Wake, 123
Jung, C. G., 11
Jungian psychology, 11–13, 47, 59

Kafka, Franz, 137
Kellman, S., 123
Kierkegaard, Søren, 5
Kitchener, Horatio Herbert, 134
Klinkowitz, Jerome, 16, 111

Lawrence, D. H.
 Aaron's Rod, 42
Lessing, Doris
 Briefing for a Descent into Hell, 111
Lukács, Georg, 124, 138
 Studies in European Realism, 137

Mann, Thomas, 124, 137
 Death in Venice, 42

Marie de France, 10, 14, 93
    Eliduc, 15, 95–96, 108
Márquez, Gabriel García, 165
Marx, Karl, 99
    Das Kapital, 68
Marxism, 138
Metafiction, 15–18, 108–10, 111, 114, 120, 125, 141
Mill, John Stuart, 68
Morris, William, 74, 88
Murdoch, Iris, 120–21, 124, 169–70

Nabokov, Vladimir, 16, 17, 124
    Lolita, 21–22
Nietzsche, Friedrich, 5

O'Brien, Flann, 15, 16
    At Swim-Two-Birds, 116, 117

Palliser, Charles, 67
Palmer, William, 34
Peacock, Thomas Love, 98
Picasso, Pablo, 96
Poe, Edgar Allan
    "The Fall of the House of Usher," 142
Pope, Alexander
    The Dunciad, 152
Postmodernism, 62–63, 68
Pre-Raphaelite movement, 74, 78

Ray, Satyajit, 124
Richardson, Samuel
    Clarissa, 29

INDEX

Robbe-Grillet, Alain, 83
Robin Hood, 28, 93, 124
Rossetti, Dante Gabriel, 74
Salami, Mahmoud, 31, 62, 64–65, 81, 83, 115, 116
Sartre, Jean-Paul, 5, 36, 42, 43, 49, 72
    Nausea, 43
Scott, Sir Walter, 124
Shakespeare, William
    Hamlet, 109, 124, 164
    Macbeth, 159
    Much Ado about Nothing, 63
    Othello, 63
    Sonnets, 112, 113
    The Tempest, 27, 28, 62–63, 140
    Twelfth Night, 63
Shaw, George Bernard
    Major Barbara, 27
Sillitoe, Alan
    The Loneliness of the Long-Distance Runner, 21
    Saturday Night and Sunday Morning, 21, 27
Sontag, Susan 67
    Star Wars, 10
Stevens, Wallace
"The Man on the Dump," 147
Sterne, Laurence, 169
Swift, Jonathan
    Gulliver's Travels, 116

Tarbox, Katherine, 51-52, 165
Tillich, Paul, 5
Thackeray, William Makepeace, 86
    Vanity Fair, 152–53

INDEX

Ucello, Paolo, 96

Victorianism, 5, 68–69,73–78

Waugh, Patricia
   Metafiction, 16, 64
Weldon, Fay, 67
Wells, H. G., 140
Whitmont, Edward, 12
Woodcock, Bruce, 35
Woolf, Virginia, 124
   Mrs. Dalloway, 107

Yeats, William Butler, 70